SOUTH KOREA
in Pictures

Alison Behnke

Lerner Publications Company

Contents

Lerner Publishing Group realizes that current information and statistics quickly become out of date. To extend the usefulness of the Visual Geography Series, we developed www.vgsbooks.com, a website offering links to up-to-date information, as well as in-depth material, on a wide variety of subjects. All of the websites listed on www.vgsbooks.com have been carefully selected by researchers at Lerner Publishing Group. However, Lerner Publishing Group is not responsible for the accuracy or suitability of the material on any website other than <www.lernerbooks.com>. It is recommended that students using the Internet be supervised by a parent or teacher. Links on www.vgsbooks.com will be regularly reviewed and updated as needed.

Note to Readers: This book uses the Revised Romanization of Korean for Korean proper nouns. Please see page 7 for more information.

Lerner Publications Company
A division of Lerner Publishing Group
241 First Avenue North
Minneapolis, MN 55401 U.S.A.

Website address: www.lernerbooks.com

web enhanced @ www.vgsbooks.com

CULTURAL LIFE
48

▶ Religion. Holidays and Festivals. Food and Dress. Visual Arts. Literature. Music and Dance. Sports.

THE ECONOMY
58

▶ Industry and Trade. Service Sector. Agriculture. Fishing and Forestry. Transportation. The Future.

FOR MORE INFORMATION

Library of Congress Cataloging-in-Publication Data

Behnke, Alison.
    South Korea in pictures / by Alison Behnke.
        p. cm. — (Visual geography series)—rev. and expanded.
    Includes bibliographical references and index.
    ISBN: 0-8225-1174-6 (lib. bdg. : alk. paper)
        1. Korea (South)—Pictorial works—Juvenile literature. 2. Korea (South)—Juvenile literature. 3. Korea—
Juvenile literature. I. Title. II. Series.
    DS902.14.B44 2005
    951.95—dc22   2004006557

Manufactured in the United States of America
1 2 3 4 5 6 - BP - 10 09 08 07 06 05

INTRODUCTION

South Korea is a small nation in eastern Asia. Lying on a slender peninsula between China and Japan, modern North and South Korea were part of a single realm during most of their history. Historically, Korea served as an important cultural bridge, linking Chinese and Japanese cultures and, at the same time, adding its own influence to ideas from both of these realms. But the nation's location also made it vulnerable to conquest, and throughout its history the peninsula fell under the rule of many outsiders. From 1910 to 1945, for example, Korea was a Japanese colony. Nevertheless, its people strove to maintain their unique traditions, identity, and culture.

In 1945 Korea's connection to the Asian mainland and to its own historical and cultural roots was severed. When the Soviet Union and the United States defeated Japan in World War II (1939–1945), they divided the unified Korea Peninsula into two separate nations. Although the two Koreas were expected to reunify eventually under a single, independent government, the philosophies of the Soviet Union

and the United States conflicted, and disagreement grew about how
the peninsula should be run. Within a few years, the brutal Korean
War (1950–1953) erupted when a Soviet-supported army in North
Korea invaded the South and attempted to reunite the peninsula under
a single Communist government. Forces from the United States and
other nations that wanted to prevent Communism from spreading
came to the aid of South Korean troops, and North Korean forces were
driven back. But the war made it clear that the division would not end
soon after all. A heavily guarded Demilitarized Zone (DMZ) was established as a buffer area between the two nations, and each began the
slow process of postwar rebuilding and recovery.

Division left South Korea with very few of the peninsula's natural
resources or developed industries, which were heavily concentrated in
the north. But in the 1960s, South Korea launched an intensive and
rapid period of industrialization. By the 1980s, incomes and living
conditions had skyrocketed for much of the population, and observers

NORTH KOREA

EAST SEA

Demilitarized Zone
(DMZ)

38th Parallel

Seoraksan
National Park

Panmunjeom

Gapyeong

GANGHWA
ISLAND

Seoul

Incheon

ULLUNG
ISLAND

Han River

YELLOW
SEA

Gum River

Daejeon

Nakdong River

Jeonju

Pohang

Daegu

Gyeongju

Gampo

Ulsan

Jangseung

Seomjin River

Namwon

Changwon

Masan

Youngsah River

Gwangju

Busan

Korea Strait

RUSSIA

NORTH
KOREA

CHINA

SOUTH
KOREA

JAPAN

INDIA

PACIFIC
OCEAN

0   900 Miles

0   900 KM

Mokpo

JAPAN

JAPAN

South Korea

——	International border
☆	Capital city
•	City
++++	Korean Train eXpress

Jeju

JEJU
ISLAND

SOUTH
SEA

0   50 Miles

0   50 KM

N

all over the world hailed the country's success as an economic "miracle."

Financial security was not the nation's only goal, however. South Koreans, having lived under a series of military dictators and governments since division, hungered for democracy. Through protests, demonstrations, and other calls for change, the people gained the right to vote freely. In 1992 voters elected Kim Young-sam, who was considered by many to be the first South Korean president elected through a truly democratic process. The nation's transition to democracy was seen by many as its second great miracle.

Yet as far as it has come, modern South Korea still faces troubling issues. Growing government corruption worries many citizens. In addition, a large number of South Koreans have long hoped for reunification with North Korea, and periodic talks between the two countries have kept that dream alive. But increasingly tense relations between the North's Communist government and the international community—especially regarding the possibility of an illegal nuclear weapons program in the North—continue to hinder reunification efforts. Nevertheless, South Korea draws on a long and rich history to help it address these challenges, and its talented and determined citizens look forward to a future that they hope will bring still greater successes.

When reading about Korea, you might notice that the same name or word may often be spelled in several different ways. These differences exist because two main methods are used for romanization (transferring Korean into the Roman alphabet used in English). These systems are the McCune-Reischauer and the Revised Romanization of Korean. Although Revised Romanization, introduced in 2000, is the nation's official system and may eventually replace McCune-Reischauer entirely, both methods remain in use. This book uses Revised Romanization.

THE LAND

Located on the southern half of a peninsula in eastern Asia, the land of South Korea is strikingly beautiful, with features ranging from rugged mountains to fertile river valleys. Almost completely surrounded by water, the country averages about 150 miles (241 kilometers) in width and 230 miles (370 km) from north to south, stretching toward Japan. South Korea's total land area is 38,324 square miles (99,259 square km), making it slightly smaller than the state of Virginia. Numerous islands dot the 750 miles (1,207 km) of South Korean coastline.

Three principal bodies of water wash against South Korea's shores. To the west is the Yellow Sea—also called the Hwang Sea or Hwanghae—which separates the country from China. To the east, between Korea and Japan, lies the Sea of Japan, which Koreans call the East Sea. To the south is the East China Sea, or South Sea, in which lies Jeju, South Korea's largest island. The 120-mile-wide (193-km) Korea Strait connects the South Sea to the East Sea.

The nation's only land boundary is with North Korea. The Military Demarcation Line, lying at the 38th Parallel of latitude, has separated the two Koreas since the close of the Korean War in 1953. A Demilitarized Zone, patrolled by U.S., South Korean, and North Korean armies, extends about 1.2 miles (1.9 km) on each side of this line.

Topography

South Korea's eastern coast sweeps southward in a nearly smooth curve, interrupted by only a few islands and natural harbors. In contrast, the nation's southern and western coasts are jagged and irregular, marked by many islands, peninsulas, and bays. This difference in the shape of the shorelines is due to geological movement beneath the ocean. The eastern coast is gradually being pushed upward, while the southern and western shores are sinking.

The shifting of the earth's crust under the ocean floor has also resulted in South Korea's mountainous landscape. In the eastern part of the country, rocky cliffs rise up sharply before dropping into the East Sea. In the south and west, hills and valleys gradually slope down to the sea, and the shores contain lowland plains. Although elevations do not reach great heights anywhere in the country, mountains make up the most prominent feature of the landscape and cover about 70 percent of the country.

South Korea's Taebaek and Sobaek mountain ranges run roughly from north to south, and the Charyeong and Jiri mountains follow a generally east-west direction. Jirisan is the highest peak on the South Korean mainland at 6,283 feet (1,915 meters), while Seoraksan (5,604 ft. or 1,708 m) in the Taebaek range is noted for its scenic beauty. Although farmers cultivate some land in the mountains, forests cover most of the area.

The 30 percent or so of South Korean territory that is not mountainous is made up of lowlands. Local farmers grow most of the nation's crops in these regions of rolling hills and plains, which lie primarily along the southern and western coasts. The majority of the country's people also live in the lowlands, especially in and around Seoul, the nation's capital and principal industrial area.

Seoraksan is reflected beautifully in a nearby lake.

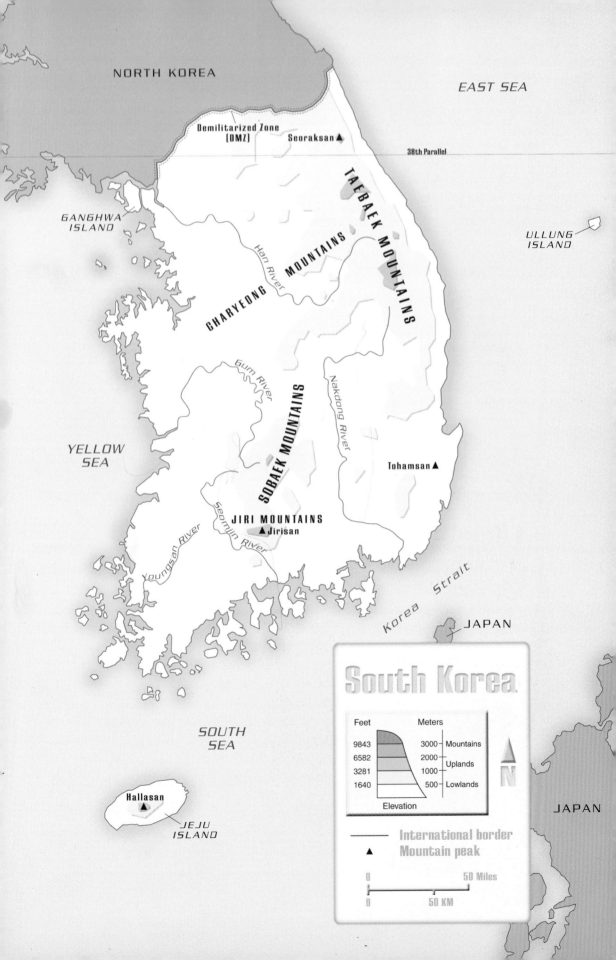

NORTH KOREA

EAST SEA

Demilitarized Zone
(DMZ)

Seoraksan ▲

38th Parallel

GANGHWA
ISLAND

ULLUNG
ISLAND

TAEBAEK MOUNTAINS

CHARYEONG MOUNTAINS

Han River

YELLOW
SEA

Gum River

SOBAEK MOUNTAINS

Nakdong River

Tohamsan ▲

JIRI MOUNTAINS
▲ Jirisan

Seomjin River

Youngsan River

Korea Strait

JAPAN

SOUTH
SEA

Hallasan
▲

JEJU
ISLAND

South Korea

Feet		Meters	
9843		3000	Mountains
6582		2000	Uplands
3281		1000	
1640		500	Lowlands

Elevation

▲ N

——— International border
▲ Mountain peak

0		50 Miles
0		50 KM

JAPAN

A field of yellow flowers blankets **the island of Jeju.** The island is famous for the *haenyo*, female divers who make their living by harvesting seaweed, shellfish, and other valuable goods from the seabed around the island. Most haenyo—who do not use scuba gear or other diving equipment—can remain underwater for up to two minutes.

Numerous islands, formed by the tips of submerged mountains, fringe the southern and western coasts of South Korea. People inhabit the bigger islands, which include Jeju, Ullung, and Ganghwa. Jeju, the largest, lies about 50 miles (80 km) south of the peninsula and covers 700 square miles (1,813 sq. km). Rising from the island is Hallasan, South Korea's tallest peak at 6,398 feet (1,950 m).

Climate

One of the primary factors affecting South Korea's weather is the monsoon. This seasonal wind blows from the south and southeast during the summer months between June and September, bringing hot, humid air to the country. Cold, dry weather comes with a monsoon from the north and northwest during the winter (December through March). Summer temperatures hover around 77°F (25°C) throughout all of South Korea. The average January temperature in Seoul is about 23°F (–5°C), while winter weather along the southern coast averages about 15°F to 20°F (8°C to 11°C) warmer. Shielded by mountains from the northwestern monsoon, the eastern coastal region also experiences warmer winters than much of the country.

South Korea receives about 40 inches (102 centimeters) of precipitation per year, nearly all of it in the form of rain. About half falls between June and August, and the rainiest region is the southern coast and islands. Precipitation levels can vary widely, however, and serious droughts occur about once every eight years. A few typhoons (Pacific hurricanes) usually pass over South Korea in late summer, bringing strong winds and heavy rains that damage crops and homes.

⊙ Rivers

South Korea's major rivers flow toward the south or west and empty into the Korea Strait or the Yellow Sea. Most of these waterways are broad and shallow. Smaller streams flow east into the East Sea and are short, straight, and fast.

South Korea's longest river, the 325-mile-long (523-km) Nakdong, rises in the Taebaek Mountains and flows southward, emptying into the Korea Strait at the city of Busan. The Han River also begins in the Taebaek range and travels west for 318 miles (512 km) before entering the Yellow Sea. Other major rivers include the Gum, the Seomjin, and the Youngsan.

The volume of water carried by South Korea's rivers varies widely between the rainy and dry seasons. During the rainy season, large dams help control flooding. These dams also produce hydroelectric power and regulate water for domestic and industrial uses. The nation's rivers are also put to good use as important sources of irrigation, and they water most of the nation's rice fields.

The Olympic Press Center in Seoul overlooks the sparkling Han River. To read more about South Korea's climate, rivers, and landforms, go to www.vgsbooks.com for links.

Flora and Fauna

The Korea Peninsula and its islands are home to many different plants. The nation's forests are filled with pine trees and deciduous (leaf-shedding) hardwoods such as maple, birch, poplar, oak, ash, and elm. Many varieties of fruit trees also thrive, including apple, pear, peach, apricot, plum, persimmon, and Chinese quince.

Above the timberline (a natural boundary beyond which trees cannot grow), the highest mountains support only alpine vegetation—tough, hardy plants that can survive high altitudes and cold temperatures. In the southern coastal regions, subtropical plants such as orange and other citrus trees are scattered across the landscape. The richest variety of plant life is found on the warm southern islands. Jeju Island has more than seventy species of broad-leaved evergreens, compared to fewer than twenty on the peninsula's southern coast.

July, as the hottest month, is the peak period for flowering plants, especially in the country's southern regions. Camellias blossom all year in the warmest areas. The rose of Sharon, South Korea's national flower, blooms from late spring to early fall.

Along with this lush vegetation, South Korean forests were once home to many large mammals, including tigers, leopards, lynx, bears, and deer. However, these animals have grown increasingly rare as humans have developed more and more areas that were once wild. Small mammals still living in South Korea include weasels, badgers, and marten. The Chinese goral—an unusual horned and hoofed animal in the goat family—inhabits mountainous areas.

One type of wildlife still abundant in South Korea is birds. About 370 species exist in South Korea, with about 50 of these types living in the region year-round and the others following a seasonal migration. The ring-necked pheasant inhabits the open countryside, where it is often sought out by local hunters. Other birds in the area are herons, larks, magpies, woodpeckers, and ducks. Additional South Korean

The **Chinese goral,** a native of the Korea Peninsula, is a rock-climbing relative of domesticated goats and sheep. They can jump to a height of 8 feet (2.4 m) from a standstill. Adults can be up to 31 inches (78 cm) tall.

wildlife includes several kinds of reptiles and amphibians, as well as freshwater fish.

Environmental Challenges

South Korea has a natural abundance of wildlife and other resources. However, periods of the nation's history—especially Japanese control, war, and the nation's rapid postwar industrialization—have taken their toll on the environment. Many of the peninsula's trees were killed during wars or were cut down for building material and to clear space for construction, leading to severe deforestation. Later, industrialization resulted in air and water pollution levels that were unhealthy both for South Korea's environment and its people.

Modern South Korea has taken steps to address these challenges. Tree-planting programs have been instituted to reforest the nation. The government has also introduced stronger regulations to combat pollution problems. These new rules have led to closer monitoring of companies' and factories' environmental records and have placed stricter limits on the output of toxic materials. However, pollution remains a problem that South Korea must continue to monitor.

Yet another environmental strategy focuses on the nation's natural areas and wildlife. The government carefully monitors visitor activity in South Korea's national parks. Areas that have been damaged by overuse or that are home to endangered animals and plants are given occasional "rest years," during which they are closed to the public. All of these measures, it is hoped, will help to preserve South Korea's natural riches.

Cities

South Korea was a primarily agriculture and rural society for many centuries. However, bustling urban life has grown rapidly as a major part of modern South Korea. The capital city of Seoul is an important world center that attracts tourists, businesspeople, and students. At the same time, valuable ruins and ancient settlements in the Korean countryside date back hundreds of years.

The octagonal (eight-sided) **Temple of Heaven,** built in Seoul in the late nineteenth century, contrasts with the skyscrapers towering overhead. Go to www.vgsbooks.com for links to learn more about urban life in South Korea.

SEOUL With an estimated population of close to 10 million, Seoul is one of the largest cities in the world. Home to more than one-fifth of South Korea's 47.9 million people, Seoul is situated on the Han River about 20 miles (32 km) east of the Yellow Sea. The city serves as the cultural, economic, educational, and governmental center of the nation.

Seoul's role as a national capital dates back more than five hundred years to the Korean Chosun dynasty which began in 1392. Under Japanese rule from 1910 to 1945, the city expanded and modernized rapidly. Although the Korean War destroyed much of Seoul, the city was largely rebuilt after the war ended in 1953, and some historical structures still stand amid modern skyscrapers. As evidence of the city's—and the nation's—growing international importance, Seoul hosted the 1988 Summer Olympic Games. Seoul was also one of several Korean cities to cohost the 2002 World Cup soccer tournament with Japan. Seoul built a brand-new stadium for the event, and tens of thousands of South Koreans—along with foreign tourists—attended the games, cheered in the streets, and gathered for parties.

OTHER MAJOR CITIES Busan, with an estimated population of 3.7 million people, is South Korea's second largest city and its largest port. Located in the southeast on the Korea Strait, Busan is the hub of South Korea's fishing industry, as well as an administrative, commercial, and industrial center. In addition, the city's beaches, hot springs, and historical landmarks attract many tourists.

About 50 miles (80 km) northwest of Busan lies Daegu (population 2.5 million), another of South Korea's largest urban centers. Landmarks in Daegu include the Dalseong Fortress, which ancient rulers built more than three thousand years ago. Daegu—the nation's largest producer of textiles—is a regional commercial and educational hub.

Incheon (population 2.5 million), situated near the mouth of the Han River, is a major seaport and handles much of Seoul's shipping. Other large communities in South Korea, such as Gwangju, Daejeon, and Jeonju, are provincial capitals that serve as local administrative centers as well as marketplaces and cultural destinations.

The South Korean port of Incheon is known for experiencing one of the world's most dramatic tides. The difference between the high and low tide can be more than 30 feet (9 m). At its lowest point, the waterline pulls far back from shore and exposes vast mudflats.

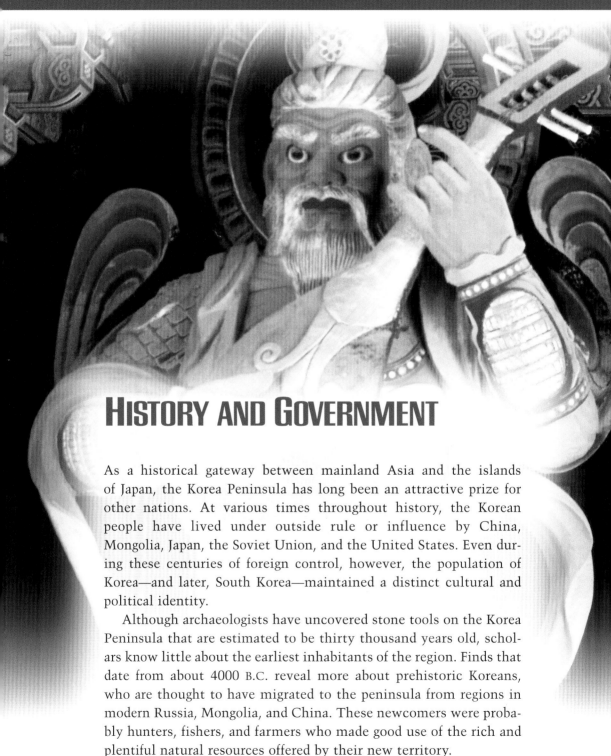

HISTORY AND GOVERNMENT

As a historical gateway between mainland Asia and the islands of Japan, the Korea Peninsula has long been an attractive prize for other nations. At various times throughout history, the Korean people have lived under outside rule or influence by China, Mongolia, Japan, the Soviet Union, and the United States. Even during these centuries of foreign control, however, the population of Korea—and later, South Korea—maintained a distinct cultural and political identity.

Although archaeologists have uncovered stone tools on the Korea Peninsula that are estimated to be thirty thousand years old, scholars know little about the earliest inhabitants of the region. Finds that date from about 4000 B.C. reveal more about prehistoric Koreans, who are thought to have migrated to the peninsula from regions in modern Russia, Mongolia, and China. These newcomers were probably hunters, fishers, and farmers who made good use of the rich and plentiful natural resources offered by their new territory.

⊳ Ancient Chosun and the Three Kingdoms

According to popular legend, a divine leader named Dan-gun founded Korea in 2333 B.C. Called ancient Chosun, meaning "Land of the Morning Calm," Dan-gun's kingdom lasted more than one thousand years. Centered in the northwestern corner of the Korea Peninsula, Chosun eventually spread northward and westward beyond the peninsula. But in the twelfth century B.C., the northern Chinese state of Yan began to increase its power, preventing Chosun from further expansion and eventually invading the realm.

Ancient Chosun gradually split into smaller units, and new states arose. In 108 B.C., the Han dynasty of China conquered northern Korea and established colonies there. Although the Chinese soon lost authority over most of the region, their influence on the Korea Peninsula remained strong for centuries. In fact, Chinese social systems were major forces in shaping the civilization and government of the region.

Around the first century B.C., several Korean groups united and formed the state of Koguryo in the northeastern part of the peninsula. Despite repeated attacks by the Chinese, Koguryo gained control of a portion of Manchuria (in modern China) and extended across the northern and central parts of the Korea Peninsula.

At the same time, other Korean states developed south of the Han River. Baekje arose in the southwest in about A.D. 245, while the Silla kingdom emerged in the southeast. Meanwhile, to the north, Koguryo also increased its strength when it took over territory from the Chinese in A.D. 313.

Each of these three major kingdoms adopted Buddhism, a religion that had been founded in India in the sixth century B.C. The Chinese brought Buddhist scriptures to the Korea Peninsula in about A.D. 372, and Koguryo accepted the new faith first. Baekje followed in 384, while Silla did not adopt Buddhism as its official religion until 528.

When Koguryo began to expand in the 500s and 600s, it came into conflict with the Sui dynasty of China to the west and with Silla to the south. Koguryo was able to repel the Sui forces. Silla leaders, however, allied themselves with the Chinese Tang dynasty. Silla's and Tang's combined forces overcame Baekje, Koguryo's ally, in 660. They went on to conquer Koguryo in 668. Famines and internal strife in Koguryo contributed to its defeat. The newly powerful Silla, like kingdoms before it, faced challenges from Chinese groups. But the kingdom successfully resisted outside rule on most of the peninsula, and unified Silla developed an advanced society and culture.

⊙ Silla Dynasty

Silla power peaked in the mid-700s, when its rulers sought to create the ideal Buddhist state. Art, literature, and science thrived and developed during this period. In addition, new policies distributed land more equally among peasants. In return, farmers gave rice, millet, barley, and wheat to the government.

Silla's capital city at Gyeongju prospered. The "bone-rank" system—a social structure based on bloodlines—gave a small group of people a great deal of power and importance. However, these highly-positioned residents enjoyed their comfortable lives at the expense of the common people, who often worked as slaves. The easy, luxurious lifestyle of the rich violated the teachings of Buddhism, which emphasizes simple, peaceful living and modest habits. As a result, the role of Buddhism as the state religion began to falter. Furthermore, conflict arose among various wealthy families who sought to gain the throne or the administration of a district for themselves. Before long, Silla began to weaken from within.

This **Silla dynasty statue** is a bronze likeness of Buddha from the 900s. The statue is 8.4 inches (21.5 cm) tall. To find out more about the long and colorful history of the Korea Peninsula, go to www.vgsbooks.com for links.

By 900 Silla had split apart into three main kingdoms. These realms fought for control of the Korea Peninsula until 936, when Wang Keon, the leader of one of the main regions, unified them once more.

The Koryo Kingdom

Under Wang Keon, the Korea Peninsula was ruled by a single kingdom again. Wang Keon named the region Koryo—from which the modern name "Korea" is derived—and extended the state's northern boundary to the Yalu River (in modern times, the border between North Korea and China). Along this northern border, Koryo forces frequently clashed with Manchurian troops from 993 to 1018. But Koryo held its position and established peace with Manchuria in 1022.

Koryo culture peaked in the eleventh century. Buddhism inspired scholarly work and art, and the ceramics industry produced beautiful celadons—pottery with a bluish green glaze. Later, the rise of printing in China encouraged the Koryo dynasty to pursue printing and publication, and Koreans invented the world's first movable metal type in 1234.

In the twelfth century, however, Koryo's stability began to crumble, as powerful families fought with the king for political control. In 1170 military leaders rebelled, frustrated that they did not rank as highly as did other government officials. The soldiers seized power, and later kings served only as symbolic rulers with little authority.

Troubles worsened further in 1231, when Mongol warriors swept into Koryo from the north and overcame the kingdom. The powerful Mongol emperor Kublai Khan, also hoping to conquer Japan, enlisted Koreans in his expeditions. The Japanese repelled the Mongolian forces, but Koryo remained under the Mongols' domination.

After 1350 Japan and Koryo came into contact again, as Japanese pirates attacked the Korean coast with growing frequency. Yi Song-gye, a Koryo military commander, defeated the raiders in a series of battles. Along with this victory, he also gained influence in Koryo's politics.

In 1368 the Chinese Ming dynasty conquered the Mongols, who had also invaded Chinese territory. Many Koryo leaders were glad to be rid of the Mongols. But when the Ming took over Mongol holdings in Koryo, the kingdom simply faced another outside ruler. Koryo's king ordered General Yi Song-gye to attack Ming forces, but Yi thought that it would be wiser to forge friendly relations with the Ming. He revolted and turned his army against the capital. Yi seized the throne in 1392 and founded the Chosun dynasty.

◔ Chosun Dynasty

During the Koryo dynasty, a group called the *yangban* had gained control of significant portions of farmland. The yangban were a class of scholar-officials, most of whom were highly educated in Confucian thought. Confucianism, like Buddhism, was a belief system introduced in Korea by the Chinese. Based on the ideas of the philosopher Confucius, it taught a system of ethics and behavior that was based on strict class divisions, rank, and respect for authority.

The yangban collected a high percentage of crops as rent from peasants who lived and worked on the land. The peasants also paid high taxes. During the Chosun dynasty, the yangban class grew rapidly and gained more and more land, putting still greater pressure on the peasants, who formed most of the population.

Buddhist monasteries also owned large amounts of land. But the monasteries lost both economic and political power when Chosun leaders denounced Buddhism as corrupt and upheld Confucianism as the ideal model for Korean life. As Buddhism declined, Korea became a primarily secular (nonreligious) society, since Confucianism was more of a philosophy than a religion.

The greatest Chosun ruler was King Sejong, who reigned from 1418 to 1450. Sejong fostered the arts, science, and technology. He also supported education. In the 1440s, the invention of a Korean alphabet, called hangul, made written information available to more Koreans. Tax reforms and health measures also greatly improved the lives of the people.

After Sejong, however, Korea fell into the hands of less talented rulers. Bitter fights often broke out over succession to the throne, and members of the yangban competed for power and desirable offices. Corruption became widespread, as royal relatives and powerful factions increased their landholdings and wealth, while farmers faced ever-higher taxes and rents.

Foreign invasions made Korea's internal problems even worse. Attacks by the Japanese in 1592 and

MILITARY MIGHT

When Japan's navy attacked Korea in the late sixteenth century, it met its match in one of the Korean military's greatest inventions. The skilled Admiral Yi Sun-shin used *geobukseon*, or "turtle ships," to fend off the Japanese forces. Covered in overlapping metal plates that created a "shell," these ships were heavily armed and very fast, proving critical in Korea's victory over the Japanese. Many people claim that Yi invented geobukseon himself, while other historians believe that the ships existed in Korea earlier than the 1500s.

Korean soldiers defend the port of Busan against an attack by the Japanese navy in the 1590s.

1597 and by Chinese forces in 1627 and 1636 upset the economy and ruined vast tracts of farmland. Koreans drove the Japanese off the peninsula, but the Chinese armies were too strong for them to defeat. Although the Chosun dynasty continued to rule, the state began sending tribute (payments) to the Chinese emperor.

Social and Economic Upheaval

During the seventeenth and eighteenth centuries, new social and economic conditions brought about changes in Korean society. As the economy grew, a class of successful merchants arose. While barter—trading some goods for others—had been the main way of doing business in the past, money replaced barter in many commercial transactions. As merchants—some of them former peasants—became wealthier, the yangban's power declined, and common people were able to improve their social status more easily. Korean writers began to describe a society that valued equality and justice.

New schools of thought that reflected these social changes emerged during this period. One was Sirhak, or "practical learning," which combined a respect for Korean history and culture with a rejection of some of Confucianism's ideas in favor of Western science, technology, and ideas of social equality and justice. This growing interest in Western thought influenced many Koreans. Although

Confucius

Chosun officials had closed their country to all foreigners except the Chinese, hoping to protect Korean culture from disruptive influences, China itself had absorbed many European ideas about government, science, and philosophy. These ideas, in turn, came to Korea and gained the respect of some scholars.

Western religion also had a growing impact. Roman Catholicism, brought to China by Portuguese missionaries, attracted followers among Koreans, who also called it Seohak, or "Western learning." But while some Catholic beliefs—such as the equality of all people—appealed to Koreans, they clashed with traditional Confucianism and ideas such as a rigid social order and ancestor worship. Chosun officials soon outlawed Catholicism, hoping to preserve Confucian practices.

The economic and social developments that began in the 1600s and 1700s continued during the early 1800s. Although ongoing struggles for power among rival officials thwarted political reform, numerous peasant revolts were disruptive but gradually led to some improvements in the farmers' lives. In the mid-1800s, a leader named Choe Che-u formed a new movement called Donghak ("Eastern learning"). This blend of religion, philosophy, and politics combined elements of Eastern beliefs such as Confucianism and Buddhism with modern ideas of social reform. The movement sought to end corruption and increase social justice within Korea.

> **Choe Che-u wanted to reach the people of Korea with the message of Donghak. However, many farmers and other workers could not read. To spread his ideas to these people, Choe set his thoughts to music and taught them as songs.**

International Involvement

Early in the nineteenth century, British ships entered Korean waters in an attempt to reach new Asian markets. By the 1840s, Russian and French merchants had also entered the region. However, the Korean government remained opposed to foreign contact. The Japanese became the first to break Korea's isolation in 1876, opening three Korean ports to Japanese trade. Meanwhile, China, feeling threatened by Japan's advances toward the peninsula, tried to reestablish its authority in the region.

Within Korea, officials and citizens split into different factions. Some wanted reform, modernization, and international contact. Nationalist groups, on the other hand, sought independence from all foreign control. Fearing that nationalists threatened the Chosun dynasty's authority, the government quickly curbed their activities. But a new challenge to the dynasty arose in 1894, when followers of the Donghak movement gathered to protest the nation's corrupt and oppressive government. Peasant armies formed, and the protests soon spiraled into a full-scale revolt later known as the Donghak Rebellion. When the Chosun king asked Chinese troops to help quell the uprising, the Japanese—still fighting for influence on the peninsula—sent in their own forces. The conflict erupted into the Sino-Japanese War, in which Japan defeated both China and the Donghak rebels.

According to the Treaty of Shimonoseki, which formally ended the war in 1895, Korea gained independence from the Chinese influence that had lasted for centuries. However, the Japanese became increasingly involved in Korean affairs and encouraged social and political reforms to prevent further internal problems in Korea.

While Japan was extending its control in eastern Asia, Russia had also begun to increase its influence in the region. In addition to taking over parts of northeastern China, Russia claimed a share of Korea's forests and mines. Resulting rivalry between Russia and Japan erupted in the Russo-Japanese War (1904). Japan won, and in 1905 Korea became a Japanese protectorate (dependent state). On August 22, 1910, Japan claimed Korea as a colony, ending the Korean Chosun dynasty.

Japanese Colonization

The Japanese government forced many changes on the Koreans. They were treated as a conquered and inferior people, and Korean culture was destroyed and covered up. For example, Seoul's name was changed to Keijo, and many of the capital's buildings were torn down and

This political cartoon shows the big arm of Japan reaching out to grasp territory in the **Russo-Japanese War (1904).** Control of the Korea Peninsula was part of the dispute between Russia and Japan.

replaced with new Japanese structures. The colonizers prevented Koreans from publishing their own newspapers and from organizing political or intellectual groups, and Japanese officials also tightened control over Korean education and shut down private schools. Many Koreans lost their land, and thousands were arrested on suspicions of working against the Japanese. Many were tortured or killed.

In 1919, in response to such treatment, nationalists seeking Korean independence organized a protest known as the March First Movement. The demonstration, which quickly expanded into a nationwide uprising, was harshly put down by Japanese forces and failed to achieve independence. However, it did mark the beginning of a national awareness and a push for freedom and democracy that unified all Koreans, regardless of social class. Over the next two decades, Korean resistance to Japanese rule grew stronger and more organized. In turn, colonial officials increased repression, and efforts to erase Korean culture continued. Colonial rulers encouraged Koreans to replace their loyalty to Korea with allegiance to Japan. A law required Koreans to worship at Shinto shrines (monuments to the traditional Japanese religion), and Japanese officials forced Koreans to adopt Japanese names. Teachers began to use the Japanese language and to focus on studies of Japanese history, culture, and other subjects. Speaking Korean was forbidden.

Meanwhile, Japan's military power and its hunger for new territory grew during the 1930s. Korea became the base for Japan's planned invasion of China, and Korean youths were drafted into the Japanese army. In preparation for this planned warfare and growth, Japan also expanded the Korean economy. Farming was increased to meet the Japanese demand for more rice, and large-scale industry grew. Economic growth, however, benefited the Japanese who controlled

SCHOOLGIRL PATRIOT

One of the most famous members of the March First Movement was a teenaged girl named Yu Kwan-sun. Born in South Chungcheong Province (in modern South Korea) in about 1904, she was away at school when the movement against Japan began. She joined protests in Seoul before returning home to help lead the uprising there, and she is said to have lit a fire on the slopes of a nearby mountain peak to signal other revolutionaries that the demonstration was beginning. When the movement was suppressed, Yu was arrested, imprisoned, and eventually tortured to death. She is deeply loved in South Korea as a national heroine, and memorials, shrines, statues, and yearly services honor her memory.

Korea, not the Koreans. By the 1930s, half of Korea's rice was going to Japan while many Koreans starved. With the outbreak of World War II in eastern Asia in 1941, conditions worsened. During the war, Japan and Germany fought against the United States, Great Britain, China, and other nations. Koreans experienced shortages of food staples such as rice, and Japanese oppression increased.

Division of Korea

Japan was defeated in 1945, and the war's victors promised Korea its independence. The United States and the Soviet Union, both on the winning side, agreed to divide the work of getting the nation back on its feet. They also temporarily divided the Korea Peninsula itself near the 38th Parallel of latitude. Expecting to stay only long enough to help the newly independent country get up and running, Soviet troops occupied northern Korea and U.S. troops remained in the South.

Koreans were grateful to be free of Japanese rule, but new challenges soon emerged. During the next two years, the two occupying powers worked toward unifying the peninsula—a goal shared by Koreans on both sides of the temporary dividing line. However, conferences between the United States and the Soviet Union deteriorated into mistrust, as U.S. and Soviet interests conflicted in other parts of the world.

In 1947 the North and South each began setting up separate governments. Meanwhile, the United States submitted the unification problem to the United Nations (UN), a newly formed international organization for handling global disputes. The UN offered to supervise elections in Korea to choose one government. But when the Soviet Union refused to allow

COLD SNAP

The Soviet Union and the United States had been on the same side in World War II, but soon afterward a political conflict known as the Cold War began. Named because it never erupted into a "hot," or military, war between the two nations, the conflict pitted Communist and non-Communist nations against each other, as each struggled to gain power and influence. The United States and other non-Communist countries tried to discourage Communist influence and feared that Communist nations would work together to take over non-Communist territory. The Cold War was one of the main reasons that the Korea Peninsula remained divided after World War II, as North Korea became a Communist state under Soviet influence.

During the **UN-supervised elections on May 10, 1948,** residents of Seoul line up to vote in private booths.

UN representatives into the North, the South held elections alone in 1948.

The newly elected National Assembly in the South drew up a constitution. On August 15, the South formed the Republic of Korea, headed by the new president, Syngman Rhee, and with Seoul as the capital. The following month, Communists in the North announced the formation of the Democratic People's Republic of Korea. Both governments claimed to represent all of the Korea Peninsula.

The Korean War

Between 1948 and 1950, North and South Korean troops clashed along the 38th Parallel several times. Despite this tension, the United States and the Soviet Union withdrew their troops in 1948 and 1949 to allow for reunification. But when U.S. defense forces left the country, North Korean leaders saw an opportunity to occupy the entire peninsula and establish it as a unified Communist state. On June 25, 1950, Soviet-supported North Korean troops invaded South Korea.

Within a few days of the invasion, the United States and other members of the UN sent military forces to South Korea. Initially, the North Koreans took over the entire peninsula up to the Busan Perimeter—a curving line of defense to the north and east of Busan. U.S. soldiers, led by U.S. general Douglas MacArthur, made a surprise landing at Incheon on September 15, 1950. Isolating North Korean troops fighting at the Busan Perimeter from those north of Incheon, the move changed the course of the war. U.S. troops then pushed on northward beyond the 38th Parallel, hoping to reunify the peninsula under a democratic, non-Communist government. But Communist China sent troops of its own to North Korea's aid, and South Korea's army was forced to retreat, arriving south of Seoul in early 1951. Although the South Koreans regained their capital a few months later, they did not make any other major advances during the remainder of the war.

Truce talks began in July 1951, but fighting continued for two more years before the opposing forces settled on a cease-fire. South Korea gained about 1,500 square miles (3,885 sq. km) of territory. A permanent peace treaty was never signed, however, and U.S. forces remain in South Korea to discourage open warfare. A 2.4-mile-wide (3.9-km) buffer area called the Demilitarized Zone divides the two sides.

The war exacted a huge toll in human lives and in property damage, leaving about five million South Koreans homeless and tens of thousands dead, and inflicting $3 billion in damage. It also left deep emotional scars on the Korean people, who began to realize that the division of their homeland would last much longer than they had hoped. In the years following the war, leaders on each side made

At the **Panmunjeom cease-fire talks** on October 11, 1951, U.S. Marine Corps colonel James Murray Jr. *(center right)* initials maps showing the northern and southern boundaries of the Demilitarized Zone. Across the table from Murray, Colonel Chang Chun-san, representing North Korea, does the same.

President Syngman Rhee struggled to lead war-scarred South Korea after the Korean War ended in 1953.

occasional attempts to discuss reunification. However, tensions and mistrust still run high on both halves of the peninsula.

Rebuilding and Corruption

The division of the peninsula had left South Korea with few industries, and the Korean War had only aggravated economic problems by destroying crops and factories. Domestic affairs disintegrated further in the late 1950s, as President Rhee's administration was suspected of corruption. His public support dropped dramatically, and when he won the presidency again in 1960, protesters accused him of rigging the elections. Mass demonstrations, led mostly by students, forced Rhee to step down, and newly elected government officials took office in July 1960. But turmoil and economic difficulties continued, and rival groups began to struggle for political power.

In May 1961, General Park Chung-hee led a military overthrow of the government and took power. Park and a military junta (ruling committee) led a dictatorship until 1963, when—under pressure to end the army's rule—Park retired from the military. He soon began working to turn around South Korea's economy by developing transportation, industry, and foreign trade. Park also introduced reforms to boost South Korean exports, and the recovering nation was soon on the road to becoming a major economic force in Asia and beyond.

But while Park and his political party won elections in 1967 and 1971, accusations of corruption and protests against the military's continued influence continued. As time went on, Park began to limit civil liberties such as the freedoms of speech, the press, and assembly, and he jailed his opponents, claiming that too much criticism might weaken the government and invite attack from North Korea.

Dissatisfaction with Park grew until October 1979, when Kim Jae-kyu—head of the Korean Central Intelligence Agency and an old enemy of Park—assassinated him.

 Visit www.vgsbooks.com for links to websites offering more detailed information about the Korean War and its aftermath, including the modern history of South Korea and its efforts to peacefully reunite with North Korea.

Struggle for Democracy

In the wake of Park's assassination, the military took full control of the government once more, in a coup led by General Chun Doo-hwan. Thousands of South Koreans protested the military's seizure of power, and in 1980 a violent clash broke out between the army and demonstrators in Gwangju. Killing at least two hundred people, the event came to be known as the Gwangju Massacre. In response, Chun soon resigned from the military and officially became president. A new constitution allowed the president to maintain strong executive powers but limited him to one seven-year term.

Despite Chun's efforts to silence opposition to his government, critics calling him a dictator remained active and vocal. At the same time, student demonstrators began to push more strongly for reunification and for the removal of U.S. military bases. Some protests turned violent, such as those at Incheon in May 1986 and at Konkuk University in Seoul the following fall.

In 1987, in response to such protests, South Korea instituted a new, more democratic constitution and held direct, universal elections. Roh Tae-woo, a former military leader and also the candidate supported by Chun, won the election—despite many South Koreans' opposition to another military president. During the next few years, Roh's government loosened restrictions on free speech and free press. Roh also broke new ground by making major efforts to build a friendlier

TROOPS AND TENSION

The presence of U.S. military bases and troops in South Korea has been an ongoing subject of controversy since the 1980s. Some South Koreans believe that this presence slows reunification efforts. In addition, some U.S. soldiers have committed violent crimes against South Koreans—especially against women. Outcry against these crimes has been widespread, and calls for U.S. withdrawal from the country have grown over the years.

South Korean university student protests against U.S. military presence in their nation reached a new peak in August 1988, the month before the Summer Olympics started in Seoul.

relationship with North Korea. He proposed ideas for trade, family visits, and security agreements between the two Koreas. In 1990 a series of diplomatic talks between northern and southern prime ministers took place. However, Roh's government was also involved in several public scandals related to the influence of bribery on ministers and other government officials.

In December 1992, South Koreans elected Kim Young-sam as their next president. Kim was not a member of the military. He was the leader of the ruling party, and he was peacefully elected president through direct elections. As a result, he was considered the first civilian president to be democratically elected in South Korea. Acting on his campaign promises, he soon began a sweeping anticorruption drive. By 1993 his efforts had resulted in the punishment of hundreds of government, military, and business officials. But the spiral of corruption continued in 1995 and into 1996. A wave of scandals spread through the government as high-ranking officials admitted to having received bribes and other illegal funding. In 1996 public trials of former presidents Roh Tae-woo and Chun Doo-hwan convicted them both of corruption, related in part to their participation in the 1979 coup and in the 1980 action against demonstrators in Gwangju.

Economic problems also surfaced in 1996 with the proposal of new labor laws. The changes allowed employers to lay off large numbers of employees if necessary, while in the past, workers rarely had to worry about losing their jobs. Public demonstrations and the largest organized strikes in Korean history erupted across the country in protest. Meanwhile, a security scare began in September of that year when a North Korean submarine entered South Korean waters.

Challenges and Change

As the wave of corruption and scandal continued to wash over South Korea throughout 1996 and into 1997, many people lost confidence in their government. Although upcoming presidential elections offered hopes of a turnaround, they quickly faded as the nation's economy took a sudden turn for the worse. Large companies collapsed or neared bankruptcy, and the government was forced to seek financial help from the International Monetary Fund—an act that many South Koreans found shameful. Amid this gloomy atmosphere, Kim Dae-jung won the presidency in December 1997.

Renewed strikes and demonstrations broke out in 1998 over ongoing economic worries, and corruption scandals came to light again in 1999. South Korean leaders sought to address the problems with further political and economic reforms in 2000. Meanwhile, President Kim worked to improve relations with North Korea, in the hopes of future reunification. Kim and North Korean leader Kim Jong-il met at a summit in June 2000, marking the first time a South Korean president had visited the North. Images of the two leaders shaking hands were seen around the world, and the historic event was a major factor in awarding Kim Dae-jung the Nobel Peace Prize that year. But reunification would be very expensive for the stronger, wealthier South. It would probably have to take on economic responsibilities including renovating the North's rundown factories, rebuilding its infrastructure (basic systems such as transportation and energy distribution), and helping to feed and house its people. Following the financial crisis, many South Koreans wanted Kim to focus on problems within the country, rather than on reunification goals.

Nevertheless, North Korea would not leave the picture anytime soon. In early 2002, a group of twenty-five North Koreans defected (illegally

Finishing public **murals of the two Koreas' leaders,** Kim Jong-il of North Korea *(left)* and South Korean president Kim Dae-jung *(right),* South Korean high school students express their high hopes for the June 2000 summit meeting. The summit was part of Kim's program of improving relations between the South and the North, which was known as his "sunshine policy."

emigrated) to South Korea with stories of famine, a repressive government, and fear. But whatever sympathy South Koreans may have felt for the people of North Korea, they gained new reason to distrust that country's government in June 2002, when North and South Korean ships off the coast engaged in a sudden, deadly battle. Each country's government blamed the other for the incident, which left at least four South Koreans dead. Hopes of peace between the two nations crumbled once again. Optimism fell even further with charges that the South Korean government, along with the large automotive Hyundai Corporation, had paid more than $1 billion to the North—essentially bribing Kim Jong-il to attend the 2000 summit.

In December 2002, Roh Moo-hyun was elected as South Korea's president. He came into office pledging to renew the fight against corruption and had many supporters among young South Koreans, who saw him as strongly pro-democracy and committed to strengthening ties with North Korea. However, he also faced a potential crisis, as worldwide concern grew over the suspicion that North Korea was developing nuclear weapons, in violation of international treaties. Hoping to defuse the situation, North and South Korea held talks in January 2003 but failed to resolve the issue.

As the world continued to follow the nuclear threat, South Korea also struggled with internal challenges. Minor scandals emerged in 2003 over illegal campaign funding. In addition, in February 2004, Roh announced a controversial decision to send South Korean troops to

Iraq, which international troops were helping rebuild and providing stability following a U.S.-led war against that country.

In March 2004, Roh's opponents in the National Assembly shocked the country by impeaching the president on charges of incompetence and of breaking election rules. Prime Minister Goh Kun stepped in as acting president, and Roh was suspended. But Roh still had an extremely loyal following, and most South Koreans believed that the charges against Roh were not serious enough to justify the impeachment. Suspecting that Roh's political rivals had used the impeachment as a nonviolent coup, tens of thousands of South Koreans took to the streets in protest. In April, while the country's Constitutional Court reviewed the impeachment, voters again showed their disapproval of Roh's opponents by giving Roh's political party many seats in the legislative elections. Finally, in mid-May, the court chose to return Roh to office. Many South Koreans welcomed his return, hoping that it was also a sign of greater future stability.

However, South Koreans were shocked to learn in late June 2004 that Kim Sun-il, a South Korean working in Iraq, had been taken hostage there by terrorists believed to have connections to al-Qaeda, an Islamic terrorist group. A video was broadcast showing Kim with his kidnappers, who threatened to kill him within twenty-four hours if South Korea followed through on its decision to send three thousand troops to Iraq. Despite widespread protest, President Roh declared that his government would not negotiate with terrorists. Kim Sun-il was executed the next day, sparking an even greater outcry against the South Korean government, as well as against the United States.

Amid the mourning and controversy surrounding Kim's death, North-South talks resulted in plans for a friendlier climate between the nations. Both sides agreed to reduce propaganda (ideas spread with the aim of enforcing a desired mindset) along the DMZ. Even more welcome to many South Koreans was the news that the United States planned to pull more than 12,000 of its troops out of the country— about one-third of the total stationed there.

Inter-Korean relations, however, suffered a setback in July 2004, when South Korea granted entrance to more than four hundred North Korean defectors who had been in hiding in Vietnam after escaping the North. The unusually large group highlighted the rising number of defectors since the early 2000s, due to deteriorating conditions in the North. But North Korea condemned the act, claiming that its citizens had been kidnapped, while officials in the South stated that the new arrivals were refugees seeking asylum. Outside observers praised South Korea's acceptance of the group, yet hoped that the issue would not threaten future talks between the Koreas.

Government

According to the Republic of Korea's 1987 constitution, executive power belongs to a president, who is directly elected by citizens for a single five-year term. All South Koreans twenty years of age or older may vote. The president, in turn, appoints a prime minister, who then helps choose fifteen to thirty members of the State Council. These members head government departments and assist the chief executive. The other main governmental body is the National Assembly. Members of this one-house legislature are elected to four-year terms. At the regional and local levels, governors, mayors, and other officials are elected every four years.

South Korea's judicial branch is headed by a supreme court. The chief justice and other judges who make up this body are appointed to six-year terms by the president. Below the Supreme Court, courts of appeal hear cases that are disputed after being tried in one of the country's district courts. The Constitutional Court handles cases specifically related to interpreting the South Korean Constitution.

The **puppies at play on the Blue House lawn** are a gift from North Korea. Their names are Dangyol (Unity) and Jaju (Independence). Just as the U.S. president's official residence is called the White House because it is white, the South Korean president's home is known as the Blue House for its blue-tiled roof.

THE PEOPLE

With a population of about 47.9 million people, South Korea is one of the most crowded countries in the world. Its overall population density is 1,251 people per square mile (483 people per sq. km), compared to 487 people per square mile (188 per sq. km) in its neighbor North Korea and 78 people (30 per sq. km) in the United States. And because so much of the country is mountainous, the true population density in major centers such as Seoul and other cities is even higher. In fact, about 79 percent of the nation's people live in urban areas. To curb a rapidly growing population, which has little room for expansion, the government started a family planning program in 1962 to limit the average family size. Since then the nation has cut its annual growth rate to about 0.7 percent, down from a peak of almost 3 percent.

The vast majority of the nation's population is ethnically Korean, as very few foreigners live in South Korea. But while South Koreans share a common language, culture, and background, their exact eth-

nic origins as a people are uncertain. Most scholars believe that
South Koreans are descendants of nomadic peoples from Mongolia.
Over the centuries, despite frequent outside rule, the ethnic mixture
of peoples living on the Korea Peninsula has remained largely
unchanged.

Nevertheless, many traits of the lives of the Korean people were
changed by outside influences. The South Korean way of life bridges
the divide between ancient traditions and modern ways, as well as
between regional and Western ideas. Most people in large cities have
adopted newer customs, while life in the countryside remains, in
some ways, the same as it has been for thousands of years.

Social Structure and Family Life

When Western influence first reached Korea in the 1600s, the
nation had a rigid social structure that was defined primarily by
Confucianism. Within this framework, individuals and social groups

were defined by their status relative to each other. For example, members of the small upper classes—which included scholars and government officials—were considered superior to lower classes, whose much larger numbers included small-scale farmers, merchants, craftspeople, and slaves. Lower classes were expected to obey and respect the higher classes.

Bowing the head is a customary South Korean greeting. The depth of the bow depends on the age, gender, education, and other status markers of each person involved. Find out more about South Korean social customs by going to www.vgsbooks.com for links.

These social conventions extended to the family, which is the first and most important element in the Korean social organization. In some cases, particularly among the wealthy, a traditional household included extended family such as grandparents, aunts, uncles, and cousins. In addition, families historically provided individual members with money, social rank, and far-reaching connections that included distant relatives. Family line and position determined an individual's place in society. The family, therefore, was valued more than the individual.

According to the Confucian model, social status—both within the family and beyond—was based primarily on generation, age, and gender. The Korean family revolved around the father, and the father-son relationship held the most importance, since the son would head the family after his father's death. Korean children and youths were always expected to respect and honor their elders. Women held the lowest positions, were responsible for almost all of the child-rearing duties, and very rarely worked outside the home.

The three most common Korean surnames (last names) are Kim, Lee (sometimes spelled Yi or Rhee), and Park (sometimes spelled Pak). In Korea the surname appears before the given name. In addition, the given name usually has two syllables. For example, Kim Dae-jung has the surname Kim and the personal name Dae-jung.

As Western ideas entered Korean society, many customs and attitudes changed, and they continue to evolve in modern South Korea. Family ties are still the most important in the society, and respect for parents and other elders remains strong.

A **South Korean bride and groom** may wear Westernized clothing for their wedding yet have a traditional Korean ceremony in many other respects.

But urban households usually consist of the immediate family only, without extended members—although older customs are still followed on some family farms. More dramatic changes include the large number of South Korean women with careers and the greater role of fathers in parenting. However, old prejudices still remain. For example, many women struggle with discrimination in the workplace.

Elaborate weddings are another example of changing customs. In rural areas, weddings are often traditional affairs, and parents may make all the arrangements—including choosing husbands and wives for their children. The bride and groom usually wear traditional clothing and hold a ceremony that draws upon ancient Confucian rituals. In contrast, most urban South Koreans choose their own marriage partners, and many rent pre-decorated wedding halls, where they hold large banquets. They often wear Westernized bridal gowns and tuxedos or suits. In both rural and city weddings, however, a customary gift is a carved wooden goose or duck, or sometimes a pair of them, called *gireogi*. The groom traditionally gives the gireogi to the bride's mother. The gift's origins lie in the fact that geese and ducks mate for life.

Living Conditions and Health

Traditionally, Korean homes were one-story structures made of brick or concrete blocks and roofed with tiles, slate, or zinc. A typical house had a living room, a kitchen, and a bedroom. But after the destruction of World War II and the Korean War, many Koreans were homeless or lived in crowded, run-down structures without running water or

Most modern **South Korean homes** have few chairs or other pieces of furniture. Instead, people sit on the floor, which is covered with mats and cushions. Visitors always take off their shoes—but keep their socks on—when entering a South Korean home.

other basic comforts. Thanks to the rapid economic growth that began in the early 1960s, however, living conditions improved dramatically in South Korea in the decades that followed. By the early 2000s, most South Koreans—especially those who lived in larger towns and cities—inhabited newer apartments or houses, and almost all homes had water and electricity.

As living conditions have improved, so has the health of South Koreans. A life expectancy that stood at 47 years in 1955 has risen to 76. Similarly, the number of infants who die in the first year of life has fallen to 8 out of every 1,000 live births—a figure that is much lower than the East Asian average of 29 per 1,000. More efficient agricultural methods and access to international food markets have also dramatically improved South Korean nutrition.

Nevertheless, health problems do remain. Poor sanitation, caused by factors including contaminated water and inadequate sewage systems, threatens both urban and rural populations. Industrial waste and agricultural fertilizers have polluted the country's land and water. Industrial air pollution has contributed to a rise in respiratory diseases such as tuberculosis, bronchitis, and pneumonia, which are some of the leading causes of death in South Korea. Seoul and other

KEEPING COZY

Since as long ago as 300 B.C., a heating system called *ondol* has warmed Korean homes. In this system, stone pipes under the floor carried hot air from the kitchen fire. The ondol system is still used in modern homes, and may use electricity, natural gas, steam, or coal to generate heat. The warmest spot on the floor is traditionally given to guests.

Better nutrition has helped many South Koreans live longer, healthier lives than previous generations. In addition to food grown in South Korea, diverse foods from abroad are available in **Seoul supermarkets.**

major cities, where pollution is especially serious, have begun tackling these unhealthy conditions.

The country's health agencies are also monitoring cases of human immunodeficiency virus (HIV) and the disease it causes, acquired immunodeficiency syndrome (AIDS). HIV/AIDS has not spread widely in South Korea, but a lack of education among most South Koreans could lead to more cases in the future. Health agencies are also closely watching for severe acute respiratory syndrome (SARS), a highly contagious, deadly illness that has been periodically widespread in Asia since 2002. South Korea has not been badly affected so far.

Steps are gradually being taken to address these health problems. To help people receive treatment when they need it, a system of medical insurance was founded in 1977. By the year 2003, the National Health Insurance Program covered 97 percent of the population, while the remaining 3 percent received coverage from the Medical Aid Program for low-income families.

A street vendor sells **traditional medicines** at an open-air market in Namwon in south-central South Korea. An open reference book invites shoppers to learn more about his products.

In Gampo in southeastern South Korea, **middle school students** leave school at the end of a long day of classes.

But while urban medical facilities are well developed, South Korean leaders are still working to extend full health care to rural areas. Also, many South Koreans seek out traditional treatment instead of or in addition to Western medicine. To address this trend, the government is trying to monitor the quality of traditional care and to ensure that traditional healers have access to supplies, education, and facilities.

Education

Education has a long history in South Korea, dating back to the first Dae-hak—"great school," or university—founded in A.D. 372. However, until the late 1800s, only the male members of a wealthy upper class in Korean society called the yangban attended school. This tradition changed at the end of the nineteenth century, when Christian missionaries opened schools that offered education to more Koreans, including women.

Under Japanese rule from 1910 to 1945, the school system changed again. Instructors began offering technical courses that prepared Koreans to work in an industrialized society. At the same time, however, the Japanese severely limited educational opportunities in other

PUT TO THE TEST

The biggest event of a South Korean student's schooling is the competitive college entrance exam. Many go to "cram schools," starting as early as junior high, to help prepare for them. It is almost impossible to cheat, since the workers who write and print the test are confined to a hotel for up to one month before the test to make sure none of the questions are leaked. On the day of the test, which is given each winter, shops and offices open later to prevent traffic jams as thousands of students travel to exam sites, and television news shows report on the progress of the test throughout the day. To keep test takers from being disturbed, drivers are forbidden to honk their horns and airlines are encouraged to change their schedules for the day.

areas. They closed private schools, strictly controlled the curriculum, conducted classes only in Japanese, and focused on teaching Japanese culture and history. Many Koreans remained illiterate during this period.

After World War II, rebuilding and modernizing the educational system was one of the many challenges facing South Korea. Achieving this goal began immediately with the establishment of the Ministry of Education. This office's duties included overseeing courses, funding, enrollment, and other administrative matters. Schools also resumed teaching in the Korean language, and the nation's literacy rate jumped from 22 percent in 1945 to about 98 percent in the early 2000s.

All children in modern South Korea are technically required to attend nine years of free primary and middle school. Many also advance to the three-year high school program. Beyond this secondary schooling, institutes of higher learning include four-year colleges and universities and two-year junior and vocational colleges. More than one-half of high school graduates go on to colleges and universities. These include Seoul National University, Yonsei University (also in Seoul), and Pohang University of Science and Technology in Pohang.

Language

Korean began as a distinct language, and it has remained largely separate from the languages of Korea's neighbors China and Japan. Most linguistics experts group it with other languages that originated in the Altay Mountains of central Asia. This category also includes the Mongolian, Turkish, and Finnish tongues.

However, the Korean language is not completely uniform. For example, various dialects exist throughout the country. The official language used in South Korea is modeled on the dialect spoken around Seoul, but most South Koreans can easily understand all of the country's dialects except for the unique version used on the island of Jeju.

In addition, as a result of Chinese cultural influence throughout much of Korea's history, Korean borrows more than half of its vocabulary from Chinese. And until the invention of the Korean alphabet, hangul, during the reign of King Sejong in the fifteenth century, Koreans wrote using Chinese characters. While the Chinese alphabet contains thousands of characters, hangul consists of ten vowels and fourteen consonant sounds, which are arranged in syllables rather than in words. After hangul was developed, it largely replaced Chinese characters in Korea. Considered one of the most logical writing systems in the world, hangul made reading and writing easier for all Koreans, and literacy increased dramatically after its introduction.

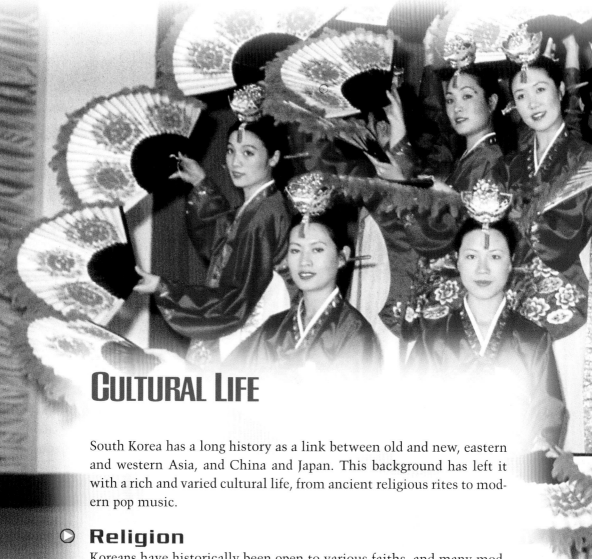

CULTURAL LIFE

South Korea has a long history as a link between old and new, eastern and western Asia, and China and Japan. This background has left it with a rich and varied cultural life, from ancient religious rites to modern pop music.

○ Religion

Koreans have historically been open to various faiths, and many modern South Koreans borrow practices from more than one set of beliefs. In addition, it is not uncommon for members of the same family to practice different faiths. South Korea's major religions and ethical systems are shamanism, Buddhism, Confucianism, and Christianity.

Shamanism is the oldest belief system on the Korea Peninsula. Early Korean shamanists, most of whom were hunters, fishers, and farmers, worshipped nature gods and ancestral spirits. They believed that the universe and everything in it were sacred and that each part of nature—from the sun and moon to rocks and trees—contained a

divine spirit. In ancient Korean history, shamans (priests) were powerful members of society and often became kings. These shaman-kings
held the double roles of religious and political leaders. Later, however,
as shamanism was joined and overshadowed by other belief systems
during the centuries, its priests lost status.

Nevertheless, many modern South Koreans still follow certain
shamanistic traditions. The most common practice still in use is the
gut, a ritual made up of dance, song, and prayer. Shamanism teaches
that negative spirits can possess people and make them sick or
unhappy. Shamans perform the gut to release these spirits.

Buddhism and Confucianism came to Korea from China, arriving
between the fourth and seventh centuries A.D. Buddhism was founded
in India in the sixth century B.C., by Siddhartha Gautama (Buddha). In
general, Buddhists believe that the path to peace and happiness is
through rejecting attachment to worldly possessions and by leading a
life of virtue and wisdom.

IN THE CARDS

Many South Koreans of all faiths seek guidance about the future from fortune-tellers. Fortune-telling is an old shamanistic tradition, and the job was once held primarily by elders in rural areas. Some people believe that true fortune-tellers are called to that profession by the spirits. But many of modern South Korea's sixty thousand or more fortune-tellers are young, work in Seoul or other cities, and choose the career themselves. Some run profitable websites and phone services, and "zodiac cafés"—where you can get tea or coffee along with a psychic reading—are also popular. Typical questions focus on jobs, admission to universities, and marriage.

Buddhism strongly influenced Koreans until about the fifteenth century, when the Chosun dynasty (1392–1910) replaced Buddhism with Confucianism as the state belief system. Confucianism, founded by the Chinese philosopher Confucius in the 500s B.C., is a set of ethical concepts to guide behavior. Because these guidelines assume that there are no divine beings to influence human conduct, Confucianism is more of a philosophy and moral code than a religion.

Christianity first entered Korea in the 1600s, when Confucian scholars began studying the Western religion and bringing translated religious texts from China to Korea. Later, further influence arrived with Catholic missionaries in 1785 and with Protestants in the 1880s. Although the government sometimes persecuted missionaries, in part because some tended to be intolerant of other religions, the faith gained many converts. About one-quarter of modern South Korean people follow Christian denominations.

During the nineteenth and twentieth centuries, some South Koreans came to believe that the existing religions were inadequate to handle Korea's modern issues and spiritual needs. They began practicing new religions, often established by messiahs—people who claim to have received messages from a god. Most of these new faiths drew heavily on Christianity, but they also incorporated elements of shamanism and other Korean religions. They gained many followers, and the largest, the Yoido Full Gospel Church, continues to attract Sunday congregations of tens of thousands of worshippers to its enormous sanctuary in Seoul.

 Find links to websites offering more information about South Korea's religions, holidays, foods, architecture, and the arts at www.vgsbooks.com.

Holidays and Festivals

With a religiously diverse population, South Korea naturally celebrates many holidays and other special occasions. One of the oldest events still observed is Chuseok, or the Harvest Moon Festival. Said to date back to the Silla dynasty, the festival is not tied to any specific religion but reflects ancient shamanistic ideas. Because Koreans once used a lunar calendar, based on the cycle of the moon, some holidays still follow this calendar. Chuseok is held on the fifteenth day of the eighth month of the lunar year, which usually falls in the autumn. The holiday celebrates the harvest, honors the moon goddess, and is a popular time for family reunions and visits to ancestral graves. And, as in most Korean holidays, a large meal is a big part of the celebration. Special dishes such as *songpyon* (rice cakes stuffed with sweet fillings) are prepared, and some of the festive food is offered to ancestors' spirits.

Another major holiday is Seol, the lunar new year. In the days before Seol, people prepare by cleaning their homes and making holiday foods. On Seol, people dress in new clothes if they can afford them, and many families share a special breakfast that traditionally includes rice cake soup. The rest of the day is spent visiting relatives, giving

South Koreans sample **traditional Harvest Moon Festival foods.** The holiday has been observed in Korea for more than 1,200 years.

gifts, and making offerings to ancestors. Other popular activities include seesawing (for girls), flying kites (for boys), and watching the colorful and energetic Nong-ak, or farmers' dance.

Most Koreans, regardless of their religion, observe these holidays. However, other, religion-specific celebrations also take place. Buddhist traditions are honored by events such as Buddha's birthday. Observed on the eighth day of the fourth lunar month, the day is a national holiday. Schools and shops are closed, and many South Koreans visit Buddhist temples to make offerings and listen to traditional music. After dark, worshippers parade through the streets to local temples, carrying colorful paper lanterns and often led by folk musicians. At the temples, the lanterns are hung up and festivities continue late into the night. South Korean Christians celebrate Easter, Christmas, and other important holidays on the Christian calendar. On Christmas Eve, young Koreans often perform a pageant or play. Many of them also go caroling, moving from house to house of friends, relatives, and teachers, and stopping along the way for snacks and conversation. Christmas Day is usually a time for attending church services and enjoying a family meal.

A popular holiday in South Korea is Shampoo Day. On the fifteenth day of the sixth lunar month—which usually falls in June or July—the occasion brings South Korean families to the country's streams and waterfalls to wash their hair in the cool water. The tradition is said to prevent fever and other illnesses in the coming year. People also enjoy picnics and games during the day, and favorite foods for the festival include fresh fruit and wheat flour cakes.

South Korea also celebrates several political and nonreligious holidays. These include the January 1 New Year, Sam Il Jul (Independence Movement Day) on March 1, and Constitution Day on July 17.

◉ Food and Dress

Korean cuisine is famous for its spiciness and rich flavors. The main food at all Korean meals, however, is simple white rice, cooked alone or with other grains. Another staple is kimchi (pickled cabbage and other vegetables), which is often prepared to be extremely spicy. Kimchi, like rice, is nearly always present on the Korean table. Soy sauce, soybean paste, red pepper, gingerroot, and sesame oil add flavor to Korean foods.

KIMCHI

Making kimchi—Korea's most well-known dish—is simple but takes a long time. Prepare this dish several days before you need it.

5 cups green or Chinese cabbage, sliced into bite-sized pieces

6 teaspoons salt

2 tablespoons sugar

1 teaspoon to 2 tablespoons crushed red pepper flakes

¼ teaspoon peeled and finely chopped gingerroot

1 clove garlic, peeled and minced

2 green onions, finely chopped

1. In a large colander, mix cabbage with 5 teaspoons of the salt. Let stand for 3 hours.
2. Rinse cabbage thoroughly. Rinse two or three more times and gently squeeze out excess liquid with your hands.
3. Place the drained cabbage in a large glass or ceramic bowl. Add the remaining teaspoon of salt and the rest of the ingredients. Mix well. Cover bowl tightly with plastic wrap and let stand at room temperature for 1 or 2 days. Chill before serving.

Makes about 5 cups

Vegetarian dishes featuring grains, vegetables, and tofu (soybean curd) are popular in Korea. Many Buddhists are vegetarians for religious reasons, and in addition, meat is relatively costly and therefore has not made up a large part of most Koreans' diets. Chicken and fish are most common. Beef is the most popular red meat and is the main ingredient in the famous *bulgogi*, a dish of beef strips marinated in soy sauce, sesame oil and seeds, pepper, onion, and garlic and broiled over a charcoal fire. Other favorite main dishes are *shinseollo*, which combines eggs, nuts, and a variety of meats and vegetables in an artistic arrangement; barbecued short ribs or chicken wings; and noodle dishes with vegetables, tofu, or meat. Various side dishes—such as bean paste soup, steamed and seasoned vegetables, and dumplings called *mandu*—may accompany the rice and entrées.

Good table manners in South Korea include using chopsticks to eat most foods, but South Koreans consider it impolite to use them for eating rice. They use spoons instead.

Most South Koreans wear modern and Westernized dress, especially in Seoul and other cities. However, traditional Korean clothing, called *hanbok,* lives on in festive occasions. The hanbok dates back to the second century A.D., and styles have developed and varied over time. Typically, the hanbok worn by women consists of a long wraparound skirt, called a *chima,* and a short jacket or blouse, called a *jeogori,* which is tied in front with long ribbons. Men's jackets are also called jeogori, and they usually have wide sleeves and are paired with baggy trousers fitted at the waist and ankles. Sometimes Korean men also wear long overcoats. Historically, wealthy Koreans often wore brightly colored silken hanbok, while the common people wore clothes of cotton or hemp and were limited to white, gray, and other muted colors. In modern times, many South Koreans don the hanbok during Seol and other festivals, in celebration of traditional Korean culture.

Visual Arts

Murals painted on the walls of tombs more than 1,500 years ago are among the earliest works of art found in Korea. These paintings usually showed images of the deceased person, animals and nature, and historical or cultural scenes. Later, from about the fifth century until the rise of the Chosun dynasty in 1392, Buddhism became the main artistic influence in Korea. Artists carved images of Buddha—such as the one in Seokguram, a cave temple near Gyeongju—from bronze or stone. Stone pagodas (religious shrines built with sloped roofs and usually many levels) and temples were built, including the Bulguksa Temple also near Gyeongju.

One of the most outstanding Korean arts has always been ceramics. The celadon porcelain of the Koryo period (918–1392) displays intricate designs of birds, flowers, and other figures. Pottery from the Chosun dynasty is simpler than celadon, and it came to strongly influence Japanese art.

During the Chosun dynasty, Confucianism replaced Buddhism as the primary influence on the arts in Korea, and with it came greater Chinese characteristics. Scholars cultivated Chinese calligraphy (ornate handwriting) and landscape painting. In addition, less-educated artists created a uniquely Korean style of painting during this period. Folk paintings depicted the daily life of common Koreans in realistic rather than idealized settings. Some of these works reflected shamanism by portraying nature gods.

Modern South Korean art still reflects the issues and topics that are important to the nation and its people, through paintings, sculptures, photographs, videos, and other works. Artists such as Choi Jeong-Hwa and Yook Keun-Byung often draw on political themes in their work, while Bae Bien-U and Park Hyun-Ki highlight nature and its importance to South Korean culture and history.

▶ Literature

Historically, Korean literature developed on two separate social levels. Scholars and wealthy people composed poetry, while most other people cherished oral tales and songs. Among the yangban, a short lyric poem known as the *sijo* arose in the twelfth century and still occupies a distinctive place in Korean literature. These simple, expressive poems describe the beauty of nature, enjoyment of life, and philosophical thoughts. Scholars often composed sijo for special occasions, and modern South Korean poets continue to use this form.

Among common people, myths and legends inspired *pansori*, which are long ballads chanted by traveling minstrels to drum accompaniment. Three of the best-known pansori are *The Tale of Simchung*, about a devoted daughter who helps to restore

KOREAN LOVE LYRICS

The path my love took is
   speckled with tears.
Playing his flute, he began
   the long journey
to western realms, where
   azalea rains fall.
Dressed all in white so neat,
   so neat,
my love's journey's too long,
   he'll never return.
. . . .
In the weary night sky, as silk
   lanterns glow,
a bird sings laments that it
   cannot contain,
refreshing its voice in the
   Milky Way's meanders;
eyes closed, intoxicated with
   its own blood.
My dear, gone to heaven's
   end alone!

—from "Nightingale: The Journey
Home" by So Chong Ju, translated
   by Brother Anthony of Taize

her blind father's sight; *The Tale of Chunhyang,* a love story; and *The Tale of Hungbu and Nolbu,* about a virtuous youth and his wicked older brother.

Government censorship has hindered the development of contemporary South Korean literature. Nevertheless, Korean authors have always found ways to express themselves. Independence and purity have long been important themes for Korean writers. The fleeting nature of time, the pleasures of family life, and loyalty to the state are other popular topics. Modern writers frequently focus on social and political ideas. The book *The Heartless,* written by Yi Kwang-su in 1917, is generally considered the first major Korean novel. It discussed the need for preserving Korean identity under Japanese rule. After the Korean War, suffering, chaos, and confusion became common themes. The poems of Kim Chi-ha, such as "Five Bandits" and "The Story of a Sound," express anger toward government corruption and brutality. More contemporary authors include Ko Un, who has written poems, novels, and essays and is known for his liberal political views and strong support of Korean unification. Shin Kyung-suk is one of the nation's most prominent female authors, and her novels often focus on the experience of women in South Korea.

Music and Dance

Like so much of South Korean culture, the nation's music and dance draw on many sources. They have roots in Confucian rituals, court music, Buddhist chants, and folk music. Court music is slow, solemn, and complex, and its dances are stately and formal. Some court music dates back to the Silla era of the A.D. 600s or earlier, while ancient Confucian music is believed to be even older. Traditional stringed instruments include zithers such as the *geum* and the *seul,* whose strings are stretched over shallow, horizontal soundboards. Flutes and reed instruments are also heard, and drums and other percussion usually accompany the human voice to mark the beat.

In contrast to the solemn court songs, folk music is usually fast and lively, with irregular rhythms, and it is often accompanied by energetic dancing. Metal gongs, the *janggo* (an hourglass-shaped drum), and the *hyangpiri* (a loud, trumpetlike oboe) are common folk instruments.

Some modern Korean composers have drawn from themes in traditional music, but Western models have also influenced South Korea's contemporary music. The country has several symphony orchestras, opera companies, and music colleges. In addition, South Korean pop music—often called K-Pop—has gained international recognition. Stars such as Jinusean, Baby VOX, Shinhwa, BoA, and Seo Taiji have attracted wide audiences in South Korea and beyond.

For those South Koreans who are not stars but would like to be, singing in the *noraebang* is a popular pastime. Also known by the Japanese name karaoke, noraebang are private rooms where everyone gets a chance to sing well-known musical numbers to the accompaniment of taped instrumental parts.

Sports

South Koreans consider athletic activity very important, and they encourage children to join sporting events and to take part in competitions. These activities range from traditional games to modern pastimes, and include both individual and team sports. South Koreans are enthusiastic both as spectators and as participants.

Some of the most popular sports in South Korea are of Western origin. The British introduced soccer to Korea in 1882. Professional and amateur soccer teams compete each year. Baseball, volleyball, basketball, skiing, and table tennis arrived in the early twentieth century, and other athletic activities enjoyed by South Koreans include golf, archery, skating, and swimming.

Of South Korea's traditional physical activities, perhaps the best known is Taekwondo. This two-thousand-year-old self-defense martial art uses rapid kicks and punches, and its name is usually translated as "the way of hand and foot." In 2000, when Taekwondo officially became an Olympic event, South Korean athletes won three gold medals.

South Korea's Kim Kyong-hun *(left)* took home one of the world's first Olympic gold medals in Taekwondo. He went up against Australia's Daniel Trenton *(right)* in the finals at the 2000 Olympic Games in Sydney, Australia.

THE ECONOMY

Half a century of occupation, division, and war left South Korea's economy seriously disrupted in the early 1950s. Division in 1945 had left the South with most of the peninsula's agricultural resources but with few industries or mineral resources. Many refugees of the Korean War entered South Korea from the North, further burdening the South Korean economy. The costs of maintaining a large and expensive army also drained the nation's financial resources. The nation endured a difficult period of rebuilding and recovery in the 1950s.

However, before the war, Japanese colonists had laid the groundwork for Korea's economic development by expanding both agriculture and industry. After the Korean War, the South Korean government built on this foundation and began land reform and industrial development. In addition, the country was home to a large labor force that was willing to work hard. Beginning in the 1960s, South Korea experienced dramatic economic growth. By the late 1980s, the country had developed its industry and its service sector (which includes jobs in tourism, government, and retail) and had entered the international economic arena.

But in 1997, financial disaster struck. As a wave of economic crises swept through other Asian countries—an event that many observers dubbed the "Asian meltdown"—South Korea was drawn into a rapid downward spiral. Businesses collapsed, banks closed, and the value of the won—the national currency—plummeted. The government was forced to accept loans from the International Monetary Fund to pay off the nation's debts, and thousands of South Koreans lost their jobs.

Following this setback, South Korea once again set to work rebuilding and restructuring its economy. While the government had previously limited foreign investment and involvement in the nation's economy, it loosened such restrictions after the crisis. In addition, many South Korean businesses had been completely or partially owned by the government, and in 1998 these companies began to be privatized, or transferred to nongovernment control. With these changes, the nation regained its footing and was still able to look back at great overall progress by the end of the twentieth century. Between the 1960s and the 2000s, South Korea's gross national product (GNP)—the total annual value of goods and services produced by the country's citizens—rose from about $100 per person to nearly $10,000. That massive growth reflected, in turn, a vastly improved standard of living for South Korea's people.

Industry and Trade

In the 2000s, South Korea has one of the world's fastest growing industrial economies. Industry accounts for about 53 percent of the gross domestic product (GDP)—the total annual value of goods and services produced within the country's borders—and employs 28 percent of the workforce.

In the 1950s, South Korea's factories focused on making labor-intensive light industrial items, such as textiles and processed food. In the 2000s, cotton, wool, silk, and synthetic fabrics are still major exports.

However, the nation has also developed heavy industry and chemical processing plants, which together account for much of modern South Korea's total manufacturing output. The nation is among the world's top producers of ships, and POSCO—founded in 1968 as the Pohang Iron and Steel Company—runs one of the world's largest and most efficient steel plants. A huge industrial complex at Changwon produces various kinds of machinery. A large electronics industry supplies foreign markets with radios, televisions, microwave ovens, and computers. Leading companies such as Samsung, Daewoo, and LG Electronics have earned South Korea a reputation for high-quality household electronics and other manufactured goods.

Automobile production has also increased, and cars are one of the nation's largest exports, along with electronics and textiles. Several large oil refineries process crude oil, which is then used in the production of plastics, synthetic rubber, and other materials. Other products

A **South Korean factory** technician tests the inner workings of an electronic device. Electronics make up a large portion of South Korea's exports.

made in South Korea include chemical fertilizers, pesticides, paper, plywood, ceramics, and rubber tires.

Only a small amount of South Korea's industrial output comes from mining, which primarily consists of tungsten and anthracite (a high-grade coal). In fact, South Korea lacks many natural resources of its own and must import large amounts of raw materials—such as crude oil, iron, steel, and chemicals—for use in its factories. The nation exports a variety of goods, including automobiles, electronic devices, ships, and textiles. South Korean companies trade primarily with the United States, China, and Japan.

Service Sector

Following industry, the service sector makes up the second-largest piece of South Korea's GDP at approximately 43 percent. However, it claims a much larger proportion of the workforce, employing more than one-half of the nation's workers. This area of the South Korean economy expanded significantly in the late 1990s and early 2000s, and service workers hold positions ranging from bank tellers and insurance salespeople to movie theater workers and retail shop owners.

Within the service sector, tourism is one of the fastest-growing areas of the South Korean economy, jump-started in part by South Korea's status as co-host of the 2002 World Cup soccer tournament. Workers in the industry hold jobs at hotels, restaurants, museums, entertainment venues, and similar sites. South Koreans themselves have also begun traveling more in the last few decades. As a result, some tourism companies and travel agencies specialize in organizing tours outside of the nation, leading trips to other Asian countries and beyond.

South Korea's main crop, rice, is growing well in these fields near Gapyeong. For the latest news and statistices about South Korea's economy, visit www.vgsbooks.com for links.

Agriculture

Although agriculture was once the mainstay of the South Korean economy, it accounts for less than 5 percent of the GDP in modern times, and employs about one-tenth of the workforce. Less than one-quarter of the nation's land is arable (suitable for farming)—and even this land is mostly hilly or mountainous. This rough terrain makes mechanized equipment difficult to use, and as a result, agricultural methods remain largely based on manual labor. However, as more and more South Koreans have immigrated to cities to find better employment, many farms have faced worker shortages. To answer the need for labor, farmers in suitable areas are gradually beginning to use machines for planting and harvesting some crops.

More than half of South Korea's farmland is used to grow rice, the nation's principal crop. On the western and southern coasts, a combination of heat and high humidity is

> Some South Korean farmers raise silkworms, which produce the fiber from which silk fabric is made. These small but profitable creatures have been part of Korean agriculture since the A.D. 600s, when peasants raised them to produce luxury items for wealthy Silla officials.

ideal for growing rice. Farmers can plant two crops a year in these regions, often alternating rice in the summer with barley in the winter. Other significant crops include cabbages, watermelons, and potatoes. South Korean farmers also grow corn, soybeans, sweet potatoes, and vegetables such as onions, tomatoes, and cucumbers. Orchards produce harvests of apples, persimmons, and pears, and Jeju is famed for its large crops of juicy tangerines. Some farmers raise livestock such as chickens, pigs, and ducks.

Fishing and Forestry

Fishing is an important part of the economy of this peninsular nation. With a modern fleet of more than six hundred deep-sea vessels and thousands of smaller boats, South Korea is one of the world's leading fishing nations. The industry provides South Koreans not only with an important source of protein but also with a valuable export. Deep-sea fishers primarily bring in hauls of tuna, which is then processed at the ports of Ulsan and Masan. The fleet often travels to waters as far away as the African coast, and while the growing restrictions on fishing in international fishing zones has hurt the South Korean tuna catch somewhat, it still makes up a significant part of the nation's fishing industry.

In the waters around South Korea, boats pull in the pollack, squid, octopus, anchovies, crabs, and mackerel that flourish there. Aquaculture—an industry that raises edible seaweed and oysters—is also an important coastal fishing activity.

Movies—a popular and fast-growing form of entertainment in South Korea—draw large audiences to local theaters, especially on holiday weekends. The most traditional movie snack in Korea is dried squid, although moviegoers also munch on candy and popcorn.

Forestry, on the other hand, is a less reliable source of income and employment in modern South Korea. Although the Korea Peninsula once lay under a thick covering of forests, most of its trees had been cut down by the early 1900s. Although Japanese colonists began reforestation efforts, hoping to reap large harvests, war brought these programs to an abrupt halt. The South Korean government set a new reforestation program in motion after the fighting ended in 1953, and the ongoing project has dramatically increased the volume of timber growing in the nation. Limiting the amount of timber that is harvested also helps control flooding and soil erosion, which are made more frequent and more harmful by a lack of trees. Nevertheless, as South

Korea's large population continues to draw on the nation's resources, deforestation remains a troubling environmental issue.

Transportation

Despite the fact that South Korea is one of the largest car manufacturers in the world, most citizens of this crowded country do not own cars. However, a well-developed public transit network provides transportation within and between cities. Buses and trains run frequently on more than 55,000 miles (88,512 km) of roads and nearly 2,000 miles (3,219 km) of track crisscrossing the country. Further expansion of both expressways and railway tracks is also planned. Urban residents of Seoul, Busan, Daegu, and Incheon often use these cities' subway systems, and many people in rural areas get around on bicycles.

In April 2004, South Korea's first high-speed train opened. Called the Korea Train eXpress (KTX), the system's trains can travel at speeds of at least 185 miles per hour (298 km per hour), and the routes run from Seoul to Mokpo in the southwest and between Seoul and Busan in the southeast. Major stops along the way include Daejeon, Gwangju, and Daegu.

South Koreans also make use of the airports located throughout the country. Korean Air, a privately owned company and the nation's largest airline, flies to major cities within South Korea as well as to destinations in Asia, Europe, the Middle East, and the United States. Like all businesses in South Korea, the air travel industry suffered setbacks after the 1997 financial crisis and the 2001 terrorist attacks in the United States, but the industry has gradually recovered. In 2001 a new international airport opened at Incheon, and in late 2003 Korean Air expanded its business beyond passenger travel and cargo shipping to include the manufacturing of aircraft and other aerospace products.

The Future

South Korea has overcome many obstacles to become the economic success and modern member of the international community that it is. The Korea Peninsula's division in 1945 and the destruction of the Korean War left the nation with a very uncertain future. But since then, the country has built up a thriving economy based primarily on industry and services. It has moved from military dictatorships to democratic elections. In addition, South Korea's involvement in world politics has brought it onto the global stage as an important player.

But challenges still lie ahead. Corruption in the government and in business has been rampant, and government censorship is also an ongoing issue. Many South Koreans worry that the democracy for which they fought so hard may be at risk. And reunification with North Korea remains one of the nation's most hotly debated topics. Some South Koreans believe that it is the only way to achieve true and lasting democracy on the peninsula. Others worry that the monetary costs of reunification would be too high, as South Korea's economy is much stronger than that of North Korea and would bear the heavier burden. On top of this concern, North Korea's possible illegal development of nuclear weapons—and international alarm surrounding the issue—have cast a dark shadow over relations between the two nations. In fact, many citizens feel that the North's Communist government is actually the biggest threat facing South Korea, which continues to maintain a large army in case of future conflict.

South Korea's continued success depends, in part, upon resolving these important issues. If the country's people are able to gain greater democratic reforms, stem corruption, and agree on how—and if—reunification with the North can be achieved, the nation may well continue to prosper and to fulfill its historical role as a bridge between governments, cultures, and eras.

MAKING CONNECTIONS

South Korea's successful auto industry had been a pioneer in forging a new relationship with North Korea. In October 2003, a large indoor gymnasium, funded primarily by the South's large Hyundai Corporation, opened in the North's capital of Pyongyang. The gymnasium was designed to host events such as basketball games between teams from the two Koreas. A stream of buses carried more than one thousand South Koreans to Pyongyang for the opening ceremonies, marking the largest crossing of the DMZ since the Korean War.

Go to www.vgsbooks.com for links to the latest news from the Korea Peninsula.

Timeline

4000 B.C.	Early evidence of human civilization in Korea
2333 B.C.	According to Korean legend, Dan-gun founds Korea.
108 B.C.	The Chinese Han dynasty conquers northern Korea.
A.D. 200s	The Baekje and Silla kingdoms form.
372	Buddhism arrives in Korea by way of China. Korea's first Dae-hak (university) is founded.
668	Silla Kingdom unifies the Korea Peninsula.
EARLY 900s	Silla Kingdom fragments.
936	Wang Keon reunifies the peninsula under a new kingdom called Koryo.
993-1018	Koryo clashes with Manchuria.
1231	Mongol warriors attack Koryo.
1392	Yi Song-gye seizes the Koryo throne and founds the Chosun dynasty.
1400s	Confucianism spreads in Korea.
1418	King Sejong takes the throne.
1440s	Hangul writing system is invented.
1592	Japan attacks Korea.
1597	Another Japanese attack on Korea takes place.
1627	Chinese forces attack Korea.
1636	The Chinese strike Korea again.
1785	Catholic missionaries arrive in Korea.
1876	Japan opens Korea's markets to trade.
1894	Demonstrations against the Chosun government erupt into the Donghak Rebellion, which then escalates into the Sino-Japanese War.
1910	Japan claims Korea as a colony.
1917	Yi Kwang-su publishes *The Heartless*, regarded as the first major Korean novel.
1919	The March First Movement takes place.
1941	World War II breaks out in eastern Asia.
1945	Japan is defeated in World War II. The United States and the Soviet Union divide Korea into southern and northern states.

1950   North Korea invades South Korea. The Korean War begins.

1951   Truce talks begin among nations involved in the Korean War.

1953   A cease-fire ends fighting in the Korean War.

1961   General Park Chung-hee overthrows the government and begins a military dictatorship.

1962   A family planning program designed to slow South Korean population growth begins.

1977   A national health insurance system is put in place.

1979   Kim Jae-kyu assassinates General Park. A military coup establishes General Chun Doo-hwan as the nation's leader.

1980   Government forces kill dozens of protesters in the Gwangju Massacre.

1987   South Korea institutes a new constitution expanding citizens' rights.

1988   The Summer Olympics are held in Seoul.

1990   Political talks take place between North and South Korea.

1997   South Korea's economy takes a sharp downturn as part of the Asian meltdown.

2000   President Kim Dae-jung meets with North Korean leader Kim Jong-il. Kim Dae-jung wins the Nobel Peace Prize for this historic effort at reconciliation.

2001   A new international airport opens at Incheon.

2002   South Korea cohosts the World Cup soccer tournament with Japan.

2003   The ongoing threat of North Korea's possible nuclear weapons program draws growing international attention and criticism. North-South talks take place.

2004   President Roh Moo-hyun is impeached in March and returned to office in May. The Korea Train eXpress (KTX) opens in April. In June North-South talks result in friendlier relations between the Koreas, and the United States announces plans to withdraw more than twelve thousand troops from South Korean soil. Kim Sun-il, a South Korean businessman, is kidnapped and executed by terrorists in Iraq, sparking antigovernment protests in South Korea. In July more than four hundred North Korean defectors arrive in South Korea.

Currency Fast Facts

COUNTRY NAME Republic of Korea

AREA 38,324 square miles (99,259 sq. km)

MAIN LANDFORMS Taebaek Mountains, Sobaek Mountains, Charyeong Mountains, Jiri Mountains

HIGHEST POINT Hallasan, 6,398 feet (1,950 m) above sea level

LOWEST POINT Sea level

MAJOR RIVERS Nakdong, Han, Gum, Seomjin, and Youngsan

ANIMALS Badgers, weasels, marten, Chinese gorals, ring-necked pheasants, herons, larks, magpies, ducks

CAPITAL CITY Seoul

OTHER MAJOR CITIES Busan, Daegu, Incheon, Gwangju, Daejeon, Jeonju

OFFICIAL LANGUAGE Korean

MONETARY UNIT South Korean won. 1 won = 100 chon.

SOUTH KOREAN CURRENCY

Korean currency first came into widespread use with copper coins during the Chosun dynasty. Later, various currencies appeared during the early and mid-1900s, as Japanese colonization, World War II, and the Korean War threw the country into turmoil. In 1962 the Bank of Korea began issuing the "new won." Although 1 won equals 100 chon, chon are so low in value that they are no longer used in South Korea. Bills come in denominations of 1,000, 5,000, and 10,000 won. The more value a bill represents, the larger the bill's size. Coins are valued between 1 and 500 won. The currency depicts prominent people in Korean history as well as scenes of traditional life and historical landmarks. Special coins are sometimes minted to commemorate major events, such as 50,000-won gold coins issued for the 1988 Olympics.

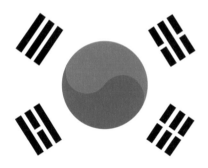

South Korea's flag, officially adopted in 1950, is called the Tae-guk-gi. The name translates as "flag of Great Extremes," and the flag's symbolism draws upon Confucian and Buddhist ideas of balance between extremes. In the center of a white background, a circle divided into red and blue sections represents yin and yang, two opposite forces that, in ancient Chinese thought, are present in all things and are both necessary for harmony. In each corner of the flag is a symbol called a trigram, from the ancient Chinese philosophical text the *I Ching*. The trigrams are pairs of opposites that expand on the yin-yang concept. In the upper left is heaven, and in the lower right is earth. Similarly, the upper right trigram represents fire, and the lower left represents water.

The South Korean national anthem, "Aegukga," has been sung since before the peninsula's division. The lyrics are thought to have been written in about 1907 by either Yun Ch'i-ho or Ahn Chang-ho, and the name means "Song of Love for the Country." For many years, the words were sung to the melody of the traditional Scottish song "Auld Lang Syne," until Korean musician Ahn Eak-tai composed new music in the mid-1930s. Although a ban was placed on the song when the country was under Japanese control, it survived and is still sung at official gatherings and other events.

Aegukga
Until the East Sea's waves are dry, and Baekdusan worn away,
God watch o'er our land forever! Our country forever!
Like a Namsan armored pine, standing on duty still,
Wind or frost, unchanging ever, be our resolute will.
In autumn's arching evening sky, crystal and cloudless blue,
Be the radiant moon our spirit, steadfast, single and true.
With such a will, and such a spirit, loyalty, heart and hand,
Let us love, come grief, come gladness, this our beloved land!

Refrain: Rose of Sharon, thousand miles of range and river land!
Guarded by her people, ever may Korea stand!

 Go to www. vgsbooks.com for links to listen to South Korea's national anthem.

The following names are written and alphabetized in the traditional Korean order, with the family name first.

AHN JUNG-HWAN (b. 1976) Ahn Jung-hwan was born in Gyeonggi Province and has loved playing soccer since he was a boy. In 2002 he rocketed to international fame after scoring a goal in the World Cup that knocked the favored Italian team out of the tournament. Married to Lee Hae-Won, a former Miss Korea, Ahn has earned the nickname "Lord of the Ring" for regularly kissing his wedding ring after making each goal. Although he has also played soccer for other countries, Ahn remains wildly popular among South Koreans and is considered their greatest soccer star.

BAE DOO-NA (b. 1979) Born in Seoul, Bae Doo-na began her career as a fashion model. When a talent scout spotted her, she got a chance to work on South Korean television shows. By the age of twenty, she had begun appearing in movies. She quickly became a favorite young actress in South Korea, with movies such as *Barking Dogs Never Bite* (2000), *Take Care of My Cat* (2001), and *Tube* (2003).

IM KWON-TAEK (b. 1936) Born in South Jeolla Province, Im Kwon-taek is one of South Korea's most famous filmmakers. In the aftermath of the Korean War, he worked as a manual laborer and later as a seller of army boots. It was not until 1956 that he got involved with film, when he moved to Seoul and met a film director who gave him a job. Just six years later, Im directed his first movie. Since then he has made more than ninety films, including *Mandara* (1981), *Seopyeonje* (1993), and *Chunhyang* (2000).

KIM DAE-JUNG (b. 1924) Born on an island off South Korea's southwestern coast, Kim Dae-jung grew up in a poor farming family. He was an outstanding student through high school, but he never went to college. The hardships of the Korean War convinced him to enter politics and fight for an honest government and greater rights. He was arrested several times for his role in antigovernment protests—giving him a reputation as a supporter of the people, which helped him win the 1997 South Korean presidential election. As president, Kim worked to restore the struggling economy. He also tried to repair the relationship between South and North Korea, efforts for which he won the Nobel Peace Prize in 2000.

KIM DUK-SOO (b. 1952) Born into a family of nine children in Daejeon, Kim Duk-soo was the son of a Namsadang, a traditional traveling musician. Showing great musical talent himself very early, especially at playing traditional Korean drums, Kim also followed this career path. As a boy, he won a presidential award for his musical ability, and he went on to attend Seoul's Korean Traditional Music and Performing

Arts School and to found the musical group Sam-mul-no-ri. Kim has also worked in theater, researched traditional Korean music, performed all over the world, and taught at the Korean National University of Arts.

KIM WOOJOONG (b. 1936) Born in Daegu, Kim began working at age fourteen to help support his family during the Korean War. Kim got a chance at a different life when he won a scholarship to Seoul's Yonsei University. Just a few years later, at the age of thirty, he founded Daewoo. Daewoo began by manufacturing textiles and has since grown into one of South Korea's largest companies, making everything from electronics to cars. Although Kim was charged with corruption during the 1990s' scandals, the story of his early hard work and great success still inspires many hopeful South Korean businesspeople.

LEE TAI-YOUNG (1914–1998) Lee Tai-young, born in what became North Korea, moved from her hometown to Seoul to go to Ewha Womans University. She hoped to become a lawyer, but in the 1940s, when her husband was targeted by the Japanese colonial government as a suspected spy, Lee had to take whatever jobs she found to support her family. She taught school, sang on the radio, and did washing and sewing. After the war, her husband urged her to follow her dream, and in 1946 she became the first woman to enter Seoul National University. She earned her law degree in 1949 and opened her own law practice after the Korean War. As South Korea's first female lawyer, Lee fought for women's rights throughout her career.

PARK CHUNG-HEE (1917–1979) Born in a village near Daegu, Park Chung-hee began his career teaching elementary school. His path changed in 1940, when he entered a prestigious Japanese military school. By 1946 he was a captain in Korea's army. He rose quickly through the military's ranks, and in 1961 he led a coup overthrowing the civilian government. After taking power, Park changed the nation's constitution to allow him to remain in office. Although he acted as a dictator until his assassination in 1979, he also made major strides to develop South Korea's economy and industrial strength.

KING SEJONG (1397–1450) King Sejong—often called King Sejong the Great—took the Chosun throne in 1418. As a scholar, poet, and musician, the young king began expanding his kingdom's horizons in these areas. He encouraged education, and his efforts led to the creation of the first Korean alphabet, greatly increasing literacy among the people. Sejong also worked to improve the lives of Korean peasants, introducing measures to ease their hardships after famines, droughts, and other disasters.

HAE-UNDAE BEACH Busan's sandy Hae-undae Beach is popular among locals and visitors alike for its beautiful view, long boardwalk, and location near natural hot springs. The beach also features a Folk Square, where beachgoers can play games, visit an aquarium, and even use a beach library.

JEJU ISLAND This lush island south of the Korea Peninsula is a beautiful natural area in addition to being an important cultural site, and it is a favorite spot for South Korean honeymooners. Attractions include ancient stone statues that dot the island, miles of sandy beaches, South Korea's highest peak at Hallasan, and a folk museum in the island's capital city of Jeju.

KOREAN FOLK VILLAGE Located about 30 miles (48 km) southeast of Seoul, the Korean Folk Village is an outdoor museum that was founded in 1974 to preserve a living snapshot of Korean history and rural life. More than two hundred structures, including houses, workshops, and a market, recreate a Chosun dynasty-era village. Various performances and demonstrations are staged throughout the village.

SEOKGURAM GROTTO Created in the 700s, this small shrine holds some of the world's best examples of Buddhist sculpture and is a treasured destination for Koreans and visitors. A manmade cave built from chunks of granite, Seokguram Grotto sits on the slopes of Mount Toham in southeastern South Korea and looks out toward the East Sea. Dozens of carvings adorn the cave's walls, leading to a domed room in which sits a large statue of the Buddha. A little way down the mountain lies Bulguksa, a famous Buddhist temple complex made up of gorgeous shrines and pagodas.

SEORAKSAN NATIONAL PARK Nature lovers won't want to miss this vast park near South Korea's northeastern coast. More than 125 square miles (324 sq. km) in area, it showcases a wide variety of natural attractions, including waterfalls, mountains, deep forest, and many miles of hiking trails. In addition, several ancient Buddhist temples are scattered throughout the park.

SEOUL South Korea's capital city offers sights for everyone. In the heart of downtown, visitors can see the modern city hall standing right next door to Deoksugung, a palace complex dating back to the 1400s. Nearby are Changdeokgung Palace and the Confucian Jongmyo Shrine. Museumgoers should check out the National Museum of Korea, which showcases a wealth of Korean art and artifacts. For a breath of fresh air, visitors can stroll in Tapgol, a large public park that was the site of the March First Movement uprising in 1919, or visit Seoul Grand Park, which contains a zoo, botanical gardens, and more. The city also offers hundreds of choices for shopping and dining.

Buddhism: a religion founded in India by the monk Siddhartha Gautama (Buddha) in the 500s B.C. Buddhism gained a following in Korea between the fourth and sixth centuries A.D.

Communism: a political and economic model based on the idea of common, rather than private, property. In a Communist system, the government controls capital and distributes it equally among citizens.

Confucianism: a system of ethics based on the teachings of the philosopher Confucius, who lived from 551 to 479 B.C., emphasizing the necessity of morality and proper conduct in all aspects of life

Demilitarized Zone (DMZ): an area that was set up in the 1950s after the Korean War to serve as a buffer zone between the two Koreas. Guards on both sides of the DMZ—which is a 2.4-mile-wide (3.9-km) strip of land along the 38th Parallel—strictly control access to the area. As an unexpected result, it has become a valuable haven for wildlife.

Donghak: a movement founded in the mid-1800s by Choe Che-u. Translated as "Eastern learning," Donghak combined religion, philosophy, and politics and blended ancient Confucian and Buddhist ideas with modern thought. Its ideas and goals included keeping Korea free of foreign influence, ending government corruption, providing more opportunities for farmers to escape from poverty and unrest, and returning to political and social stability.

International Monetary Fund (IMF): an organization of almost two hundred countries that extends loans, credit, and other economic support to struggling nations

junta: a ruling committee whose members are usually drawn from the military

nationalists: people who follow the philosophy of nationalism, which values loyalty to one's own nation above all else. Nationalist goals may include preservation of national culture, fulfillment of the nation's needs, and the nation's independence from outside influence.

Sirhak: a school of thought that arose in the 1600s. Translated as "practical learning," Sirhak emphasized the value of Korean history and culture in solving the modern state's problems. At the same time, Sirhak scholars rejected many traditional aspects of Confucianism in favor of Western science, technology, and thought.

United Nations: an international organization formed at the end of World War II in 1945 to help handle global disputes. The United Nations replaced a similar, earlier group known as the League of Nations.

Western: a geographic and political term that usually refers to the politics, culture, and history of the United States and Europe

yangban: a powerful and wealthy class of scholar-officials who were highly educated in Confucian thought. The yangban arose during the Koryo period (936–1392) and gained power and prominence under the Chosun dynasty (1392–1910). They gradually declined as internal conflict rose and as merchants and other members of Korean society achieved greater wealth and influence.

Selected Bibliography

Breen, Michael. *The Koreans: Who They Are, What They Want, Where Their Future Lies.* New York: St. Martin's Press, 1999.
Written by a British journalist who lived in South Korea for several years and still spends half of his time there, this book offers an insightful look at the Korean character and an analysis of how it has been affected by history.

Cable News Network. *CNN.com International: Asia.* 2004.
<http://edition.cnn.com/ASIA/> (April 23, 2004).
This site provides current events and breaking news about South Korea, as well as a searchable archive of older articles.

Connor, Mary E. *The Koreas: A Global Studies Handbook.* Santa Barbara, CA: ABC-CLIO, 2002.
This comprehensive text touches on topics from geography to shamanism, offering an informative and helpful introduction to South Korea.

Europa World Yearbook, 2003. Vol. 2. London: Europa Publications, 2003.
Covering South Korea's recent history, economy, and government, this annual publication also provides a wealth of statistics on population, employment, trade, and more.

Hoare, James, and Susan Pares. *The Simple Guide to Customs and Etiquette in Korea.* Folkestone, Kent, UK: Global Books, 1996.
This introduction to Korean ways offers a valuable glimpse into Korean culture, helping visitors avoid embarrassment.

Kendall, Laurel. *Getting Married in Korea: Of Gender, Morality, and Modernity.* Berkeley: University of California Press, 1996.
This fascinating look into changing Korean marriage traditions examines their meaning to contemporary Korean society, as well as women's role within that society.

Lee, Peter H., ed. *Anthology of Korean Literature: From Early Times to the Nineteenth Century.* Honolulu: University of Hawaii Press, 1981.
This book brings together sijo, pansori, and other traditional Korean writings.

———. *Modern Korean Literature: An Anthology.* Honolulu: University of Hawaii Press, 1990.
This anthology surveys twentieth-century Korean poetry, fiction, and essays.

New York Times Company. *The New York Times on the Web.* 2004.
<http://www.nytimes.com> (April 21, 2004).
This on-line version of the newspaper offers current news stories along with an archive of articles on South Korea.

Nilsen, Robert. *South Korea Handbook.* Chico, CA: Moon Publications, 1997.
This well-illustrated travel guide provides historical and cultural details along with practical information for visitors to South Korea.

Oberdorfer, Don. *The Two Koreas: A Contemporary History.* Reading, MA: Addison-Wesley, 1997.
This book covers the history of the Korea Peninsula since its division, exploring the results of the war, international politics and involvement with the Koreas, and major events within the two countries.

"PRB 2003 World Population Data Sheet." *Population Reference Bureau (PRB).* 2003.
<http://www.prb.org> (April 21, 2004).
This annual statistics sheet provides a wealth of data on South Korea's population, birth and death rates, fertility rate, infant mortality rate, and other useful demographic information.

Turner, Barry, ed. *The Statesman's Yearbook: The Politics, Cultures, and Economies of the World, 2003.* New York: Macmillan Press, 2002.
This resource provides concise information on South Korean history, climate, government, economy, and culture, including relevant statistics.

Chung, Okwha, and Judy Monroe. *Cooking the Korean Way.* Minneapolis: Lerner Publications Company, 2003.
This cultural cookbook presents recipes for a variety of authentic and traditional Korean dishes, including special foods for holidays and festivals.

Feldman, Ruth Tenzer. *The Korean War.* Minneapolis: Lerner Publications Company, 2004.
This book presents a history of the Korean War, which tore the peninsula apart between 1950 and 1953.

Ho-Am Art Museum.
<http://www.hoammuseum.org/english/index.asp>
Use on-line galleries and a virtual tour to take a peek at the collections and special exhibits of the Ho-Am Art Museum. Located about one hour south of Seoul, this major South Korean museum houses a rich array of ceramics, calligraphy, paintings, Buddhist art, and more.

Kim Dong-sung, ill. *Long Long Time Ago: Korean Folk Tales.* Elizabeth, NJ: Hollym, 1997.
This illustrated collection brings together twenty traditional stories that have been loved by Korean children for generations.

Korea DMZ.
<http://www.korea-dmz.com/en/cm/main_en.asp>
This site offers a wealth of information on the Demilitarized Zone separating North and South Korea, from history and geography to wildlife.

Korean Folk Village.
<http://www.koreanfolk.co.kr/folk/english/index.htm>
The official website of the popular Korean Folk Village presents details on traditional Korean homes, crafts, festivals, and more, as well as information on how to visit the village, located south of Seoul.

Korean Overseas Information Service. "Korean Government Home Page." *Korea.net.*
<http://www.korea.net/>
Check out information on South Korean business, arts, sports, national symbols, current events, and much more at this comprehensive site.

National Museum of Korea.
<http://www.museum.go.kr/eng/index.html/>
This highly interactive website allows visitors to take a virtual stroll through the main galleries of Seoul's National Museum, including rooms of Buddhist statues, celadons and other pottery, prehistoric artifacts, period-style rooms and furnishings, and photography.

Park, Linda Sue. *Seesaw Girl.* New York: Clarion Books, 1999.
The story of Jade Blossom, a girl in seventeenth-century Korea, gives readers an up-close glimpse of Korean life at the time.

———. *A Single Shard.* New York: Clarion Books, 2001.
This Newbery Medal-winning novel for young adults centers on Tree, an orphaned Korean boy growing up in the 1100s.

Further Reading and Websites

————. *When My Name Was Keoko.* New York: Clarion Books, 2002.
A brother and sister in Korea struggle with life under Japanese rule, during which both of them are forced to change their names.

Sherman, Josepha. *The Cold War.* **Minneapolis: Lerner Publications Company, 2004.**
This book introduces readers to the causes, events, leaders, and effects of the Cold War.

vgsbooks.com
<http://www.vgsbooks.com>
Visit vgsbooks.com, the homepage of the Visual Geography Series®. You can get linked to all sorts of useful on-line information, including geographical, historical, demographic, cultural, and economic websites. The vgsbooks.com site is a great resource for late-breaking news and statistics.

Captions for photos appearing on cover and chapter openers:

Cover: Businesspeople and shoppers bustle along a street in central Seoul, South Korea's capital.

pp. 4–5 The Changdeokgung Palace's Secret Garden covers six acres (2.4 hectares) in Seoul. It was first landscaped with woodland paths, lotus ponds, and pavilions (decorative shelters) in 1623.

pp. 8–9 Autumn colors greet hikers in the rocky upper elevations surrounding Soraksan *(center)*, a scenic mountain peak in northeastern South Korea. Many South Koreans consider autumn their favorite season, when the weather cools off and hundreds of maple trees burst into bright fall color. Jangseung, a city in the southern part of the country, even holds an annual Maple Festival to celebrate the beauty of the season.

pp. 18–19 At the Buddhist Bulguksa Temple in Gyeongju, sculptures representing each of the four Heavenly Kings—one for each cardinal direction (north, south, east, and west)—are said to permit goodness to enter the temple but keep evil out. The eastern Heavenly King *(left)* holds a *bipa,* or Korean lute, which has the magical property of allowing him to control the weather. The southern Heavenly King *(right)* holds a sword, which multiplies to match the number of enemies he is facing.

pp. 38–39 A South Korean family enjoys a day at Lotte World of Adventure, a huge indoor amusement park in Seoul. More than six million people visit the park annually.

pp. 48–49 Dancers wearing *hanbok* (traditional Korean clothing) to perform the traditional fan dance, or *buchaechum,* pose for a photograph with their pink fans open. During the dance, the fans are manipulated to look like dancing hibiscus flowers. The dancers' beauty and grace are said to attract attention the same way beautiful flowers in nature attract bees.

Photo Acknowledgments
The images in this book are used with the permission of: © John Elk III, pp. 4–5, 41; © Digital Cartographics, pp. 6, 11; © TRIP/TRIP, pp. 8–9, 10, 12, 38–39, 42, 43, 45, 48–49, 54, 62; © Art Directors/ TRIP/Antonia Deutsch, p. 13; © San Diego Zoo/Minden Pictures, p. 15; © TRIP/T. Bognar, p. 16; © TRIP/R. Nichols, pp. 18–19; © TRIP/J. Stanley, p. 21; © Korean Overseas Information Service, p. 23; California Academy of Sciences, p. 24; Library of Congress, p. 26 (LC-USZC4-8487); U.S. Army, p. 29; National Archives, p. 30; American Embassy, San Francisco, p. 31; © R. K. Hur; p. 33; © Reuters/CORBIS, pp. 35, 37, 57; © SETBOUN/CORBIS, p. 44; © Art Directors/TRIP/Trip, p. 51; © TRIP/J. Trapman, p. 61; Audrius Tomonis/ www.banknotes.com, p. 68 (all); Laura Westlund, p. 69.

Cover: © John Elk III. Back cover photo: NASA